Gods and Myths of Ancient
Greece

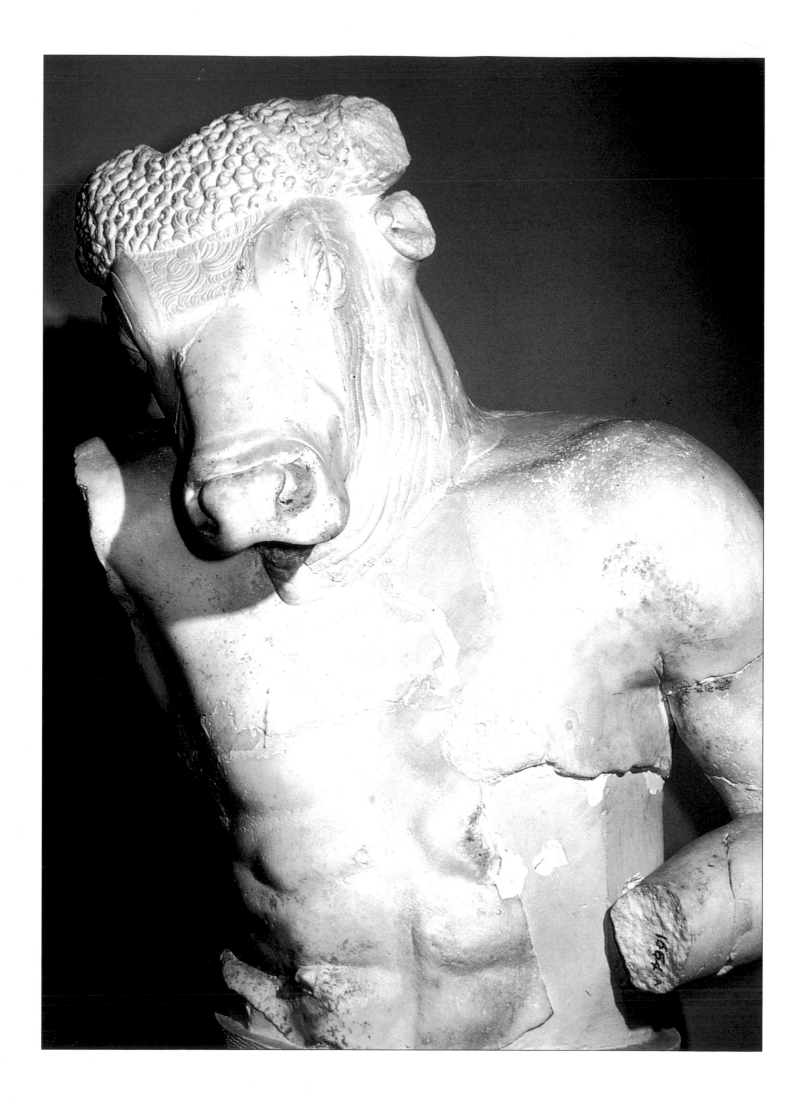

Gods and Myths of Ancient Greece

Mary Barnett
Photography by Michael Dixon

Grange BOOKS

Published in 1999 by

Grange Books
an imprint of Grange Books PLC
The Grange
Units 1-6
Kingsnorth Industrial Estate
Hoo, Nr. Rochester
Kent
ME3 9ND

ISBN 1 84013 350 3

Printed in Singapore

*Page 2: (National Archaeological Museum, Athens) The Minotaur,
Greek sculpture.*

*Page 3: (National Archaeological Museum, Athens) Greek painting
on a wood panel, from Corinth (520-500 BC). Musicians
accompany a sacrifice.*

*Above: (National Archaeological Museum, Athens) An ivory group
from Mycenae (14th-13th century BC). This triad may be connected
with legends of orphan infants brought up by two or more divine
protective nurses.*

CONTENTS

A note on the spelling of names

Although it is more usual now to spell names in a way that is closer to the Greek original, I have chosen to use the forms that will probably be more familiar to English speaking readers. Thus, for example, I have used Heracles and Circe, rather than Herakles and Kirke, and Daedalus and Oedipus, rather than Daidalos and Oidipous.

INTRODUCTION

The gods and myths of Ancient Greece still have a significant place in Western culture. The thunderbolt of Zeus, the trident of the sea-god Poseidon and the staff of Hermes are still recognizable and evocative images. We speak familiarly of the constellations of Orion, Cassiopeia and Andromeda. Modern writers can conjure up the futile heroism of war and the destruction of civilizations by mention of Troy. The heroes Heracles and Odysseus still exemplify strength and wily resourcefulness respectively, and we all know how Freud made use of the Oedipus myth. The stories of the Greek gods and heroes have been retold, reinterpreted and alluded to in the painting, sculpture, literature and music of the Western world for centuries.

This book sets out, in images and words, to familiarize the reader with some of the most important myths. It introduces the chief gods of Ancient Greece with the attributes by which they can be recognized. Then it outlines the stories of some of the most popular heroes of myth, and recounts briefly the tale of the Trojan War and the return of Odysseus. It ends with an account of the mythical stories of two of the ruling dynasties of Ancient Greece, showing how the dramatists of Classical Greece found inspiration in stories that were already ancient, and used them to explore both human morality and the relationship between gods and men.

Before exploring the myths themselves, however, the book gives a brief account of the changing civilizations from which they emerged. Myths might be described as traditional tales that have significance for the people they belong to. They are sometimes connected with early religious or social practices or ceremonies; they sometimes attempt to explain the origins of a group of people or celebrate their victory over another group; they are occasionally explanations of natural phenomena or allegories for the subordination of savage forces to rational order. Above all, they are good stories that give some shape to human experience and help people to talk about why things are as they are.

The origin of the myths is usually unknown and lies in the very distant past, long before the people who told them could read or write. Because they are stories that one generation of people told orally to another, they developed and changed in the telling according to the customs, tastes and needs of the tellers. We know them only in the form they had attained at the moment when they were written down and only in the versions that happen to have survived. The very act of writing the stories, which usually happened long after they had first been told, probably changed them yet again.

The Greek myths developed over a long period, during which a number of different groups of people inhabited the land we now call Greece. The myths include stories that probably originated in Asia, the Middle East and other parts of Europe, and to see why this is so it is necessary to begin with some account of the land, its changing population and the religion that gradually developed there before the eighth century BC.

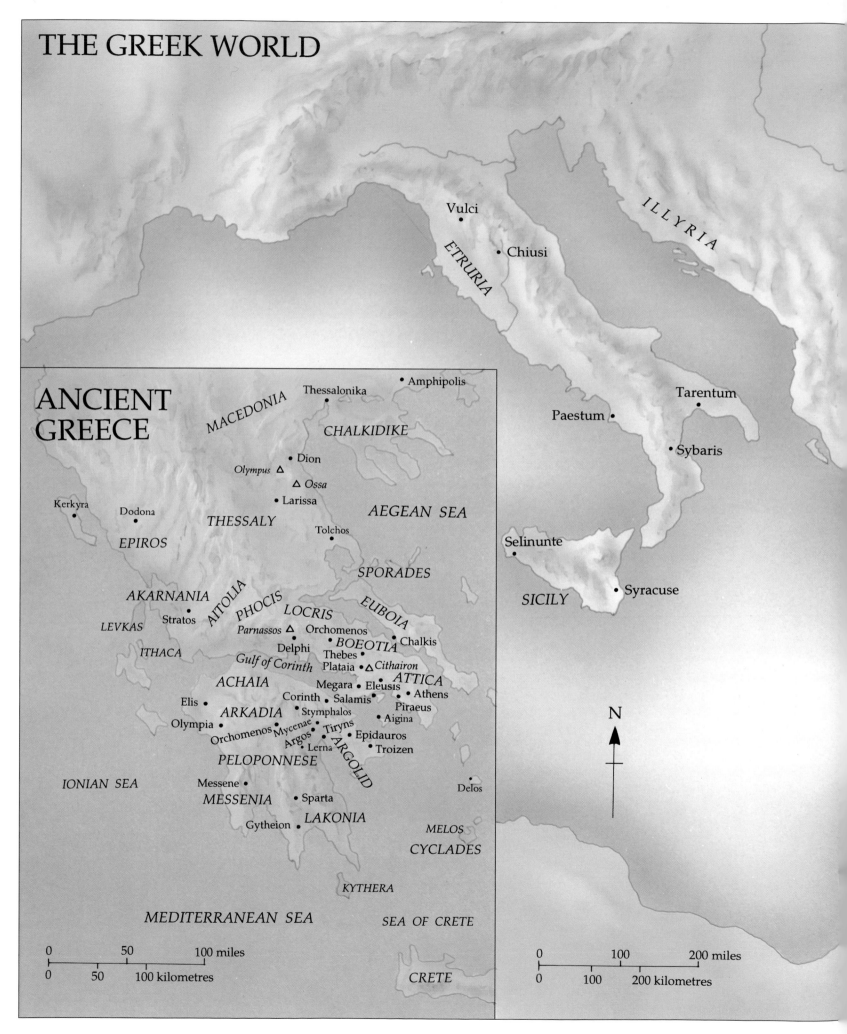

THE GREEK WORLD

Vulci

ETRURIA

ILLYRIA

Chiusi

Tarentum

Paestum

Sybaris

ANCIENT GREECE

Amphipolis

Thessalonika

MACEDONIA

CHALKIDIKE

Dion

Olympus △

△ *Ossa*

Larissa

Kerkyra

Dodona

THESSALY

AEGEAN SEA

Tolchos

EPIROS

SPORADES

Selinunte

Syracuse

SICILY

AKARNANIA

AITOLIA

PHOCIS

LOCRIS

EUBOIA

LEVKAS

Stratos

Parnassos △

Orchomenos

Chalkis

Delphi

BOEOTIA

ITHACA

Thebes

Gulf of Corinth

Plataia

△ *Cithairon*

ACHAIA

Megara

Eleusis

ATTICA

Corinth

Salamis

Athens

Elis

ARKADIA

Stymphalos

Piraeus

Olympia

Orchomenos

Mycenae

Tiryns

Aigina

Argos

Epidauros

Lerna

Troizen

ARGOLID

PELOPONNESE

IONIAN SEA

Messene

Delos

MESSENIA

Sparta

LAKONIA

Gytheion

MELOS

CYCLADES

KYTHERA

MEDITERRANEAN SEA

SEA OF CRETE

N

| 0 | 50 | 100 miles |
| 0 | 50 | 100 kilometres |

CRETE

| 0 | 100 | 200 miles |
| 0 | 100 | 200 kilometres |

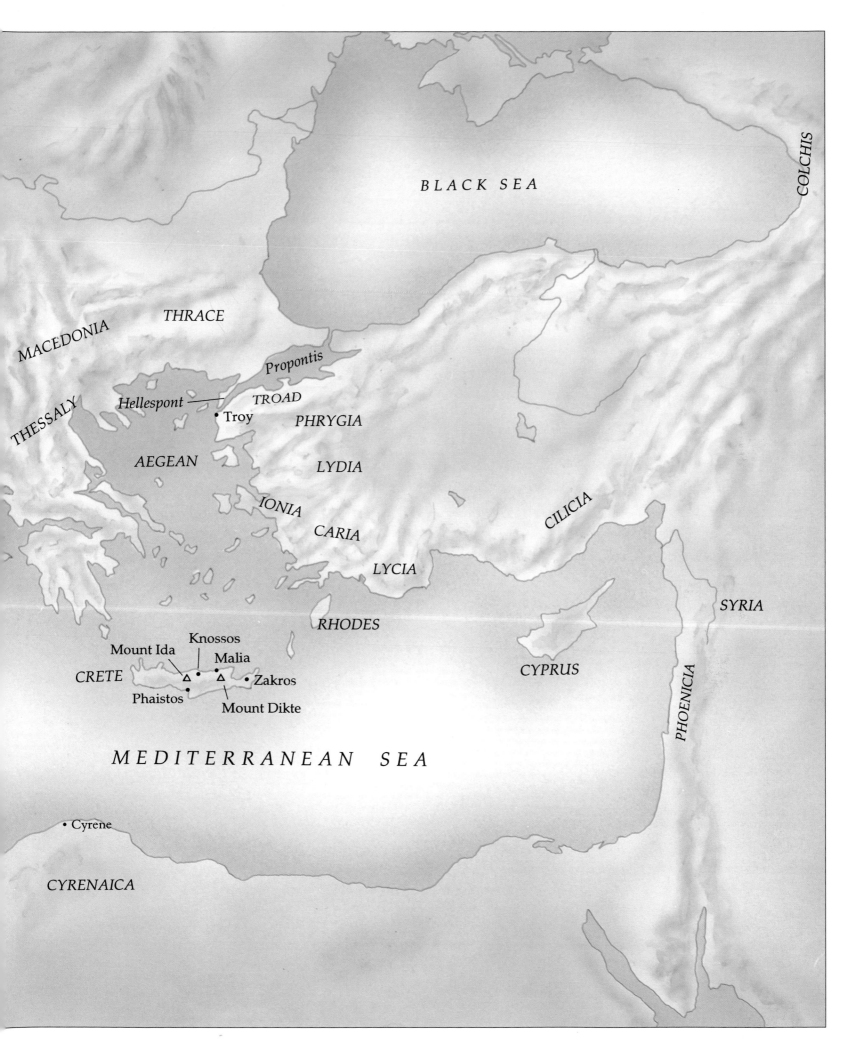

BLACK SEA

COLCHIS

THRACE

MACEDONIA

THESSALY

Propontis

Hellespont

TROAD

Troy

PHRYGIA

AEGEAN

LYDIA

IONIA

CARIA

LYCIA

CILICIA

RHODES

SYRIA

Knossos

Mount Ida

Malia

CYPRUS

CRETE

△ ● △ ● Zakros

Phaistos

Mount Dikte

PHOENICIA

MEDITERRANEAN SEA

● Cyrene

CYRENAICA

CHAPTER ONE
GREECE: THE LAND AND THE PEOPLE

ABOVE
Sunrise behind the mountainous Isle of Hydra.

OPPOSITE
A typical sheltered, fertile area edged by mountains. Mount Parnassus, once sacred to Dionysus, is in the background.

The geographical position of Greece in the ancient world was probably a crucial factor in the development of its richly varied mythology, which absorbed elements from a number of different cultures. Because Greece lies towards the eastern end of the Mediterranean, it is a stepping stone between west and east, between Europe and western Asia; groups of islands in the Aegean form a bridge between Greece and Asia Minor, and the land mass itself stretches southwards into the Mediterranean basin, towards Egypt and Libya.

Four-fifths of Greece is mountainous, or semi-mountainous, but from the mountains the sea is usually visible. From early times, the rugged nature of the terrain encouraged its inhabitants to travel more easily by sailing round the coast and from the mainland to nearby islands and other Mediterranean coastal areas. The deeply indented coastline, sheltered bays, gulfs, and archipelagoes, together with the tideless Mediterranean and unusually clear light made sea travel comparatively easy, so trade and cultural contacts with nearby maritime civilizations were established early.

Yet the cultural diversity that such contact brought to Greece was balanced by an intense and proud localism largely caused by the nature of the land itself. Since agriculture was by far the most important activity for almost everyone, population was necessarily concentrated in the scarce fertile areas: in the coastal plains, estuaries, and river valleys edged by mountains, on isolated plateaux and on the islands. It is not surprising that there was competition for these areas and that, from time to time, groups of people migrated from less favoured to more favoured land, where they formed relatively isolated but close communities. There are no great navigable rivers, and roads have to find their way round mountains. Thus when incomers brought their stories and their gods to a new area, the stories and the gods were likely, over time, to be assimilated into existing ones, to be given local significance and to be subjected to local interpretation.

Ancient Greek civilization developed with man's ability to make and use metal. In the Aegean area, the effects of the new technology of the Early Bronze Age were most obvious at first in the Cycladic Islands, but from about 2500 BC they seem to have spread throughout the area and reached parts of mainland Greece. Higher civilizations that were both urban and literate had, of course, already come into being by this time in favourable areas, to the East in Mesopotamia – in the fertile plain of the Tigris and the Euphrates – and, slightly later, to the south in Egypt – in the Nile Valley. These cultures were influential in the Eastern Mediterranean throughout the Early Bronze Age.

In the Middle Bronze Age, about 2000-1450 BC, the first European high civilization developed gradually in Crete. The archaeologist, Sir Arthur Evans, who excavated and reconstructed the Palace at Knossos on Crete, named this the Minoan civilization because of memories, preserved in the Greek myths, of stories of the great King Minos of Crete, his palace and its labyrinth.

Crete became the unchallenged and dominant naval power in the Aegean. In about 1900 BC, Minoan power within the island seems to have been centralized in a number of newly constructed palaces, some built on the sites of older ones, each of which became the focus of its surrounding area. The palaces were important administrative centres and also clearly centres of wealth and therefore of artistic and technical achievement. This period of Minoan administrative centralization and cultural growth in Crete paralleled the rise of the Hittite civilization in Asia Minor. Surviving artefacts from Crete suggest that, while the Minoan civilization was influenced by the East, it possibly had a more humane religious and artistic tradition of its own that found much of its inspiration in nature.

Its power was ended by natural disaster. Archaeologists have shown that when, in about 1500 BC, an earthquake, followed by a huge volcanic eruption, tore the island of Thera apart, submerging

half of it, the resultant tidal waves, which carried masses of exploded pumice, battered many islands in the southern Aegean, including Crete. Sometime just before 1450 BC there seems to have been another major natural disaster, and the fires that followed it destroyed virtually all the important Minoan buildings on Crete. A generation later, the palace of Knossos was re-occupied by Greek-speaking Mycenaeans from the mainland, who continued there until its final destruction in about 1375 BC.

The Late Bronze Age on mainland Greece (c.1450-1200 BC) is actually often referred to as the Mycenaean Age in reference to the rise and subsequent expansion of the Greek-speaking civilization that had been developing there, and whose population is sometimes described as Achaian, a term used by Homer. The most important centre of this civilization was Mycenae, which is in the Argolid in the north-eastern Peloponnese and was brought to light in modern times by Heinrich Schliemann in 1876.

Mycenaean culture, based on farming and stock-breeding, had long been comparatively austere. It is, incidentally, interesting in this context to note that Homer describes an early king, Odysseus, doing his own ploughing. Yet when Schliemann excavated the shaft graves of rulers at Mycenae, which date from about 1600 BC, he found evidence of great material wealth, partly in the form of golden objects. It is now thought possible that gold was brought back to Greece, in the form of wages, by Mycenaean soldiers who had fought as mercenaries for Egypt, and that the inclusion of precious objects in the graves was influenced by Egyptian burial customs.

Both the weapons and the warlike decoration of other objects found in the graves give a picture of a more aggressive civilization than that of the Minoans, and the fact that some of the skeletons were almost two metres tall adds to the impression that their owners were taller and stronger than the Mediterranean people.

After the destruction of the Cretan centres, Mycenaean influence increased in the Aegean. The Mycenaeans had assimilated certain elements of Minoan civilization, such as the method of conducting their administration from a number of powerful centres, and they learned to be sufficiently good sailors and merchants to overtake the Cretans' dominance at sea. They soon expanded their interests to the islands, to the west coast of Asia Minor and to trading posts in Cyprus. They exported their pottery, which was simpler and cheaper to produce than Minoan pottery, to southern Italy and Sicily and to Egypt. They also extended the number of their settlements on the mainland, right up to the Thessalian plain, which was horse-breeding country.

Population increased, agricultural methods improved, and there was probably a rise in the standard of living. Palaces were built at Tiryns, Mycenae, Pylos and Thebes that fulfilled an administrative function for their surrounding regions similar to that adopted earlier in Crete. Some of these centres had strongly built, fortified walls that greatly impressed a later, less developed population who attributed almost supernatural powers to their dead builders. The Mycenaeans organized a road system that connected the centres of scattered kingdoms with their outlying regions and with each other, yet legends and poetry record memories of warlike conflict between the states.

Mycenaean civilization reached its peak towards the end of the thirteenth century BC. According to

TOP
(National Archaeological Museum, Athens)
This fine bronze dagger from the royal graves at Mycenae, inlaid with gold, silver and niello, shows a lion hunt in which the huntsmen use bows and javelins and protect themselves with 'figure-of-eight' and 'tower' shields. It demonstrates the artistic and technical skills of its maker and the strength and vigour valued by the society it came from.

LEFT
(British Museum) A limestone female votary (c. 6th century BC). This is Phoenician work but was found in Cyprus, suggesting the continuity of cultural contact that was maintained between different groups in the Aegean area.

tradition, it was in those years that its rulers and young warriors undertook an expedition against Troy; indeed, epic accounts of this expedition were so deeply embedded in oral tradition that it was accepted as an historical fact by later Greeks. Nevertheless, Mycenaean civilization had almost come to an end by that period. At the end of the thirteenth and the beginning of the twelfth centuries, for as yet unknown reasons, a number of its centres in Greece were destroyed by fire, and others were simply abandoned.

At the same time, across the sea in western Asia there was a period of great instability and confusion. A number of factors led to the break-up of the Hittite Empire and this had indirect but serious consequences for the Mycenaean world. For example, the destruction of the Canaanite trading cities on the coast of Asia Minor helped to destroy Mycenaean trade with the East, so that the Mycenaeans became reliant instead on what they could grow and make at home. This in turn lessened their need for the upper layer of palace administration that had controlled foreign trade and the distribution of goods.

The consequent falling standard of living persuaded some people to disperse from mainland Greece to familiar areas of the Near East and to the islands of Rhodes and Cyprus. In Greece itself there was a movement of population away from the difficult hinterland towards the more fertile eastern and western coastal areas. As a result, the great palace centres were replaced by less powerful, less wealthy, more dispersed centres of smaller regions. These, however, still maintained some indirect contact with the East, mainly through Mycenaeans living in Cyprus.

Gradually, less advanced people from the mountains and arid plains moved southwards down the Greek peninsula to take over newly-abandoned land that was nevertheless preferable to their own. There was a consequent slow but comprehensive resettlement of population throughout Greece. Soon after 1100 BC there were no more attempts to revive foreign trade; the last acropolises were abandoned and so were some settlements that had formerly lived chiefly off trade. The Mycenaean world sank into the period of adjustment that is, perhaps unfairly, called the Dark Ages.

The migratory movements of various groups in this period, roughly between 1125 BC and 800 BC were far too complex to detail here, but they had a profound effect on the development of religion and culture in Greece. The migration, which used to be called loosely the Dorian invasion, was not a single movement as this suggests but a gradual change:

sometimes groups split up; sometimes they moved swiftly, stayed in a new area for a few decades, then moved on again. Quite large groups crossed over from the mainland to the western coast of Asia Minor, for example to the area that became known as Ionia.

The migrating groups gradually settled down and, in spite of emerging inequalities between groups and individuals, the Greek people began to share certain common beliefs and cultural standards. When the 'Phoenician' alphabet was adopted to Greek use it initiated the possibility of literacy throughout the Greek world. Although the new states and political units were smaller than those of their Mycenaean predecessors, many of them survived for centuries.

During this period, we move from prehistory to history, and the use of written records adds a new dimension to our knowledge. The written myths suggest that migrating Greek-speaking tribes had memorized early catalogues of their genealogies and explanations of their origins and that they handed down traditional stories about their settlements and their feuds from one generation to the next. Once these stories were collected and written down, they came to be treated as distant but authentic history. The so-called 'Dark Ages' were, therefore, actually crucial to the restructuring and formation of the Greek world, and it was during this period that many of the myths must have developed.

The period between about 800 BC and the Classical period that shone particularly brightly in the fifth century BC is usually called the Archaic period. One of the most significant new developments at this time was social and political. The immigrant groups had preserved their ancient organization into 'tribal states', although in many cases these no longer corresponded to specific tribes. In these states the ruler's power was derived from an assembly of warriors who supported him as long as his good fortune and physical strength assured them that he was favoured by the gods. This is the kind of state that seems to form the background of most of the myths. In the eighth century a new kind of social and political organization called the *polis* began to emerge, which moved the emphasis away from the power of the ruler towards a more collective and public responsibility.

The Greek term *polis* is difficult to define because examples of it were so variable. It is usually translated into English as 'city state', but this gives a somewhat false impression. In general terms, the *polis* was a self-ruling, autonomous community that could consist of a group of villages and some scattered settlements or might include a town. It functioned in those areas of communal life that demanded collective action, and in time it usually developed a focal point such as a town with a market and a place of assembly.

Greater stability and gradually improving agricultural methods at this time meant that some small landowners began to prosper and, as heads of families, some of them now became citizens, eligible to join local councils, which now met at stated regular intervals and made real decisions. Clearly this shifted the balance slightly between rulers and ruled. Local aristocrats, usually from a limited number of well-established families, nevertheless monopolized official positions, such as the magistracy, and so increased their political influence.

Gods and myths must have played a significant role in the establishment of these newly structured communities that were so dependent upon their members' shared sense of place and kinship. The practice of local religious cults and the telling of traditional local legends helped to define a *polis*, and loyalty to its cults would be expected of all its citizens. Archaeological evidence supports this view by suggesting that the sort of items that had normally been buried with rich individuals were from this time more commonly dedicated at civic sanctuaries, which were often sited outside the main settlement and probably maintained by communal expenditure.

These successors of the Mycenaeans, who included descendants of some of the earlier Mycenaean inhabitants of their localities, gradually caught up with the more advanced people of the Mediterranean area and, as they did so, seem to have become more consciously Greek. An important focus for this consciousness were the works of the poet we know as Homer, which were probably written down in the eighth century BC, or even a little earlier. The *Iliad* and the *Odyssey* celebrated the achievements of earlier, greater, probably Mycenaean, heroes in stories that had clearly been told and developed over several centuries before they were finally written down. For the Greeks of the Archaic and Classical periods they had historical rather than legendary or mythical significance, and aristocrats would recount genealogies that demonstrated their direct descent from one or other of the heroes who had fought at Troy. From Homer and subsequent writers the Greeks also derived a common pantheon of gods with which they were able, in many cases, to assimilate their local gods.

The development of athletic competitions formed further links between Greeks. Aristocrats dedicated much of their time to achieving and maintaining healthy and beautiful bodies through exercise. Men of this period inherited a tradition of athletic contests, which had sometimes been held originally to mark an important event such as a victory or the funeral of a hero. Such games became displays of physical superiority. In this period of the development of communal institutions, the contests became closely linked with religious festivals and holidays and could be seen as each individual's pious offering of his best efforts to the gods. Several of these games became pan-Hellenic events, notably the ones held at

(Capitoline Museum, Rome) Roman copy of a Greek imaginary portrait of the poet Homer. No authentic image of Homer exists, but this is typical of ancient perceptions of him.

Olympia. The origins of the Olympic games are unknown, but the conventional date of the first games is 776 BC, and the four-yearly event soon served as a dating system for the whole of Greece.

This period is one of expansion, when Greeks, having already settled in the East, founded colonies to the west, in southern Italy and Sicily, and this period of exploration and settlement is also reflected in some of the myths. It was also a period of great diversity among states and races, and of turmoil and revolt as men fought for a greater share of power.

Some states made notable advances: Sparta greatly increased its extent and population through military conquest, while Athens flourished economically and produced goods, such as pottery, of increasing interest and accomplishment. Sparta moved towards a democratic system of rule, but was held back by its inflexibility. In the sixth century,

however, Athens began to achieve something closer to a true democracy when it allowed small local units to control their own affairs without the interference of the aristocracy, yet to be grouped into larger units so that they felt part of the state for other purposes.

Fifth-century Athens, during the flowering of the Classical period, is the time and place most people imagine when they think of Ancient Greece. By that period the gods and myths were not only established in the popular consciousness but celebrated and recalled in writing, in dramatic festivals and in the arts of architecture, jewellery and pottery. Stories were sometimes elaborated deliberately and with artistic intent, but they were still reworkings of the mythical narratives that concern us here, which had been formed, then developed, merged, systematized and transmitted by word of mouth through the preceding centuries.

ABOVE
(Old Corinth Museum) Greek vase painting (6th century BC) shows a competitor taking part in a chariot race, an important event at the Olympic Games.

OPPOSITE TOP
(British Museum) Black figure dish from Attica (c.550 BC). The lively depiction of a hunter and his dog is typical of the fluidity of design achieved in the area around Athens at this time, when pottery was increasingly often decorated with scenes from everyday life.

OPPOSITE BOTTOM
The vaulted entrance to the Stadium at Olympia has been restored to its form of the 4th century BC. Excavation of the stadium unearthed votive offerings that had been found buried respectfully by men who had made repeated alterations in much earlier times.

CHAPTER TWO
RELIGION: FROM PREHISTORY TO HISTORY

Cycladic marble female figure (third millenium BC). This is characteristic of the flattened, schematic figures that were laid in tombs beside the dead. Their significance is not clear.

The changes in population, outlined in the previous chapter, naturally brought changes in religious belief. The religious beliefs of people in prehistory cannot be recovered with any certainty, but archaeological evidence sheds some light on their religious practices. If we begin once more in the Aegean Early Bronze Age (c.2800-1900 BC), no building has been found on the Greek mainland that can be said certainly to have been intended for a sacred purpose, whereas such buildings have been found in more Eastern civilizations dating from much earlier periods. On the other hand, graves found in the Cycladic islands at this period suggest that great care was taken over the burial of the dead, who were surrounded with personal belongings as though they were expected to need them in a life that would continue after death. It has been suggested that some of the apparently simple figurines found in the Cyclades both in settlements and graves may have represented goddesses, but there is no proof of this. Somewhat later, however, in the Middle Bronze Age (c.1900 BC-1500 BC), there is evidence for the worship of a female deity in a special sanctuary on the island of Keos.

In the Early Bronze Age, in parts of Crete, the dead were buried in small, stone, vaulted 'beehive' tombs with doorways, a long-lasting style, which later developed into the monumental *tholos* tombs that were also found in Mycenaean Greece. The care taken over such tombs again suggests belief in the after-life but perhaps more importantly a desire to honour the dead who had been important in life.

In the Middle and Late Bronze Ages (c.1900 BC-1100 BC) most evidence of the worship of deities and the particular importance of certain symbols comes from the Minoan civilization of Crete. Our ideas about Minoan religion have been deduced partly from the unusually fine objects and paintings found in Crete by archaeologists and partly from what appear to be memories of Minoan beliefs that were assimilated into Greek myths.

The number and variety of representations that have been found of a female figure suggest that the chief deity was a goddess, or a number of different goddesses. Early deities are often represented as female, and this was certainly the case in many Asian cults. The Cretan goddess appears in association with mountain peaks, with a sacred tree, with snakes, poppies and doves. Sometimes she is shown as 'The Lady of the Animals', with lions and panthers, just as the goddess Artemis was, later, in Greece. This manifestation indicated both her power over wild nature and her protective attitude towards it, as opposed to her connection, suggested by her association with trees, with the vegetation and cultivation upon which people depended for daily life. Her female nature is usually stressed in early figurines by her nakedness and later by her dress and her full breasts, which are usually shown uncovered. A young god seems to have been associated with her, possibly sometimes as her son, sometimes as her partner. It has been suggested that he was a particular representation of the vegetative aspect of nature, since he was born, died and came to life again each

year. He too has parallels in earlier Asian cults.

Minoan worship and art seem to have been intimately connected with the natural world, which is scarcely surprising at a time when agriculture and the capture of wild game were obviously the basis of life. Joy at bringing in the harvest is expressed so vividly by the singers engraved on the vessel known as the 'Harvester's Vase' that it cries out to us today. At some of the palaces, such as Malia and Zakros, a type of circular altar called a *kernos* with hollows all round the rim and a larger hollow at the centre has

been found. It is thought that such altars were used to make multiple offerings, probably of cereals, with oil in the centre hollow, and that they might have represented the 'first fruits' of the land.

There is a good deal of evidence to suggest that caves and mountain peaks and certain trees, pre-eminently the useful olive, were treated as sacred. For example, in the Cave of Eileithyia near Amnisos, named after a goddess of reproduction, a large and a smaller stalagmite were apparently perceived as representations of the goddess and her child, since their

votaries, or worshippers, built a low wall, which still exists, round the stalagmites, and left vessels there. These were likely to have been filled with oil or honey since tablets inscribed with Linear B script have shown that the Cave of Eileithyia was one of the places to which olive oil and honey were distributed as religious offerings by the Palace of Knossos.

Small figurines, representing the votaries themselves, have been found in the Diktean Cave, which was thought by the Greeks to be the place where their goddess Rhea hid her new-born son Zeus. Bronze double axes, an important symbol to the Cretans, were found with swords in a cave near Arkalochori, which was presumably felt to be the home of a warlike divinity. Sanctuaries were also built on some mountain peaks.

Rooms that appear to be shrines have been found in houses and palaces, and in late Minoan times what seem to be communal sanctuaries began to appear. It is possible that the king and queen themselves represented the deities at palace shrines, and received offerings in their place. Some memory of royal participation in religious ritual is perhaps suggested by the stories in Greek myths of King Minos of Crete and of his wife Pasiphaë.

The bull occupied a central place in Cretan culture, its original importance presumably being simply that it supplied meat, leather and dung, and inseminated the dairy herds. In some Eastern religions the bull deity is identified with the heavens and the sun, while the sacred cow is associated with the moon. Cretan art presents us with numerous lively representations of bulls, especially in the public sports where athletes appear to have seized the bulls' horns and somersaulted the length of their backs. There are images of bulls being sacrificed, and bulls' horns had symbolic significance for the Minoans, apparently being used to mark off certain areas of the palaces.

From such evidence it seems likely that early Mycenaeans had also adopted a goddess of vegetation and fertility and there are images of a goddess as 'The Lady of the Animals', who would have been important to the Mycenaeans who were hunters and stockbreeders. Some clay figurines show a stylized goddess with her arms raised in an attitude of benediction. There is no evidence that the Mycenaeans adopted the Cretan snake goddess, however. As a more warlike civilization, they made images of a goddess of war, not as a woman but in the form of a palladion, or shield-like standard made in the familiar figure-of-eight shape of early Mycenaean shields, with a female head projecting from the top of it and a spear from its side. It seems likely that the early shield was itself the significant symbol of a cult connected with war.

Engravings on jewellery suggest that the Mycenaeans, like the Minoans, regarded the tops of hills and mountains as sacred places and built small cult shrines there, decorating their façades with bulls' horns, which were an important symbol for them also. Although Mycenaean religion borrowed some elements from Crete, it is likely that it actually originated elsewhere and that its tradition was essentially closer to the Greek religion of historical times that we shall examine next.

The centuries that followed the end of Mycenaean palace civilization are 'dark' in the sense

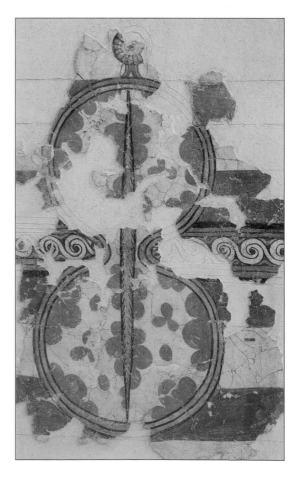

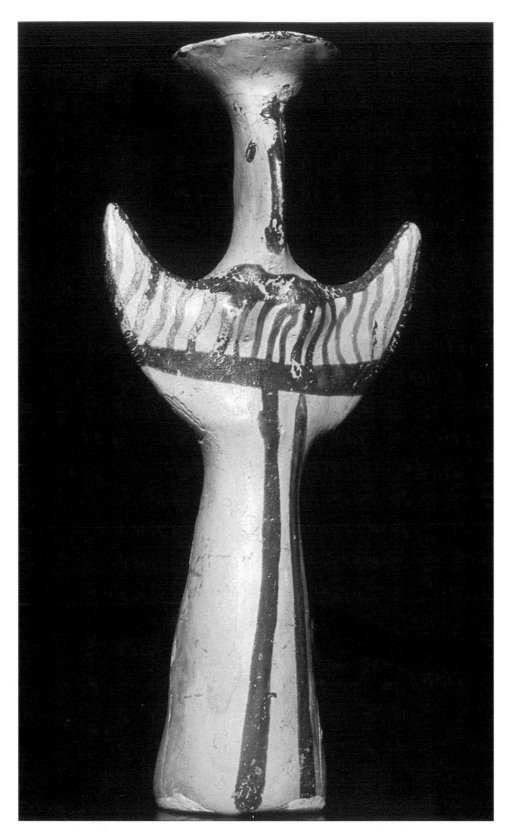

The decipherment of Linear B script on Mycenaean tablets from Knossos has shown that some Olympian gods, including Zeus, Poseidon, Hera and Hermes, were already being worshipped by the Mycenaeans in the fourteenth and thirteenth centuries BC and had been taken by them to Crete at the end of the Minoan period. It is, however, difficult to discover much about the beliefs of the Mycenaeans, and knowledge comes chiefly from small statues and from carvings on jewellery and seal stones.

that so little is known about them, yet they were crucial in forming the religion that we now recognize as Ancient Greek. The gods of this religion emerge to clear view in the works of Homer and Hesiod sometime in the eighth century BC (although some people now place Homer in the second half of the ninth century BC) and they will be described in detail in the following chapters.

The gods who lived on Olympus had, in some respects, a recognizable family life, although in most respects an extremely irregular one. The structure of the Olympian pantheon was probably a simplification and reduction of belief as it actually existed among the population at large in the eighth century, yet it was important in that it served to give some sort of uniformity and consistency to Greek religion right through to the Classical period and beyond.

Its polytheism implied that different gods had different spheres of influence and that all of them could be worshipped by a pious person because each god had influence over a different aspect of human life. At the same time, it was perfectly possible to pay particular attention to one god. Worship of one god did not exclude worship of the others. There was no single correct belief, only correct religious practice.

Neither was there a single origin of this religion, as has been demonstrated. The only god whose name it seems possible to reach back to with any certainty

is that of Zeus himself, the sky god, whose name probably originates from an Indo-European word. Since the language of the Greeks suggests that they were once Indo-European speaking, such an origin for their most important god seems obvious. The origins of the other deities cannot be determined simply. It must be remembered that the Bronze Age inhabitants of Greece had contacts with the ancient civilizations of the Near East. Then, after the end of the Mycenaean palace period, new Indo-European speaking tribes, probably having beliefs of their own, moved southwards into Greece. Some earlier inhabitants moved away and resettled on the west coast of Asia Minor, where they were subject once again to new influences because Asian cultures had also undergone change over time. These influences had an effect, in their turn, on the population of mainland Greece.

During the period of the settlement of new tribes and the resettlement of the existing population in Greece it seems that both groups were broadly tolerant in religious matters. As incomers settled into new areas, they seem to have accepted the deities that already existed there as well as sometimes importing new ones. The long period between the ending of Mycenaean civilization and the clarification of belief we see recorded in the works of Homer was therefore one of adjustment, of assimilation of new rituals to old ones, of the merging of different but often probably closely related deities. In time, the local gods became subsumed into the Olympian pantheon, possibly because the Olympians carried more prestige.

It is because of this readjustment that the gods often have more than one name, are described by different epithets, are shown with different attributes and have so many myths associated with them. Many of their epithets and attributes demonstrate local claims on a god of the pantheon, or encapsulate memories of an earlier god who has been assimilated with one of the Olympians. Sometimes an epithet merely indicates the aspect in which the worshippers wish to appeal to the god on a particular occasion, thereby encouraging an important generalized deity to focus on a small, particular need that might once have been served by a special, local god. It was considered important to address a god correctly by the name that would best enlist his help in a particular function.

The number of female partners attributed to some of the male divinities probably reflects the need to subordinate powerful, early, local female deities to newer, male gods.

The new settlers in Greece would have been

introduced to existing sacred places where divinity was felt to be present, where cults were practised, offerings made, or perhaps shrines or sanctuaries were built. Sometimes these were the sites not of major divinities but of some minor supernatural figure, such as a local spirit of nature, a nymph, or a hero. As on Crete, sometimes stones or trees were themselves felt to be sacred.

Hero cults tended to be particularly localized, and were often focused on an early tomb or a place where some event of local importance, such as a vic-

(British Museum) Greek terracotta seated figure from Boeotia. Such terracotta figures were produced in large numbers and usually had a votive function, representing the deity of a specific sanctuary. Boeotia was particularly active in their production.

RIGHT
The impressive landscape surrounding
the Sanctuary of Apollo at Delphi.
In the foreground is a marble tholos,
or rotunda, built in the early 4th century BC.
Its dedication is unknown and it is one of the
many buildings that accumulated over
the centuries at this particularly sacred site.

tory in battle, had occurred. It is important to remember that the telling of myths and stories of heroes provided a history for people who had no recorded past, and that aristocrats, in all seriousness, charted their descent from gods or heroes. The migrations of people meant that it became particularly important to be able to establish divine authority for a group's presence in and rule over their new locality, and this was sometimes achieved through stories of a local, tribal god who was said to have emerged from the earth itself. Yet in spite of population changes, there was often continuity of worship at ancient shrines. There were sometimes changes in the identity of the deity being worshipped, but respect was usually shown by the incoming group to the beliefs of those who had gone before.

Once the Olympian theological system had been established it became possible for groups all over Greece to share it, at least at the level of common public belief. Places that had long been held as particularly sacred became accessible to everyone. Among these were the great sanctuaries whose remains we can still see. What impresses the visitor to Greece today is the beauty of many of these sites. It is easy to understand how divinity could have been felt to inhabit their very rocks and trees.

The sanctuary at Delphi was already the most important religious centre in Greece, and was in fact regarded in antiquity as the centre of the world. It was originally sacred to Gaia, or Ge, the earth mother, but it later adopted the cult of Apollo, and was later still also associated with Dionysus. Like other cult areas it would originally have been just an open precinct with an altar and perhaps a simple, representational statue of the cult figure. Later, a large temple was built to house a statue of the god and gradually other buildings clustered on this uniquely important site. From the eighth century BC it was normal for a religious site of any importance to have a temple with a cult image inside it – a home for the god rather than a place for communal worship; the sacrificial altar would stand in front of the temple.

The great sanctuaries were unusual in maintaining a priesthood, and it was to the Delphic priesthood that city states turned for advice on religious matters, such as the acceptance of foreign cults. Rulers of states and individuals all approached the Delphic oracle for advice.

There were many sanctuaries where methods of divining the future were practised and to which people turned for advice and guidance. There are numbers of myths concerning the Delphic oracle, but in historical times prophecies seem to have been given by a series

of venerable women, each called the Pythia, as they sat on the sacred tripod inside the temple of Apollo. The sanctuary at Dodona long remained simply an open-air precinct, where the priests heard the oracles of Zeus in the sounds of the wind-blown leaves, or the metal cauldrons that they hung in the branches of the trees. Small tablets have been found there on which people inscribed their questions for the god, and these show how directly and intimately religion and daily life were connected.

The sanctuary at Epidauros gave revelation in a different way. People who were sick visited this shrine dedicated to Asclepius, a healing god, and spent the night in special rooms at the sanctuary until the god sent them a curative dream. Inscriptions have been found there that tell the stories of specific cases of dreams that induced healing.

Each city probably had its own cult, and some of these attained a pan-Hellenic importance. A few became popular mystic cults whose celebration was more personal and intense than usual and which differed from the normal forms practised on behalf of the people by their rulers and aristocratic magistrates in being more concerned with death and the after-life than the here and now.

One of the most important of these was the cult of Demeter at Eleusis. This was probably a very early rural cult in origin, celebrating the corn-goddess, Demeter, and her daughter, Kore – 'the maiden' – later called Persephone. Demeter is said to have rested at Eleusis during her search for her lost daughter, who was being held in the Underworld. Her cult developed into the Eleusinian Mysteries, to which men were initiated by means of secret teachings, and which were said to offer great consolation and revelations about life, death and the after-life.

In about the sixth century BC, another cult arose that attached little importance to earthly life but suggested that men must prepare themselves for greater happiness in an after-life. Followers of this cult were called Orphics, probably after Orpheus who went down to the Underworld to bring back his wife Eurydice from the dead, but had her snatched from him again when he turned to look at her as they neared the entrance to the world of the living. Orphics saw the body as a prison in which the soul, which had once been happy, was confined for some fault that the owner of the body was unaware of. At death, the soul had atoned for its fault, and was free to return to the blessed land – unless the owner of the body led an unjust life, in which case the soul was imprisoned in another body until full atonement was made.

Another rural cult that became a popular ecstatic cult and moved into cities was that of Dionysus, which is thought to have come from Asia through Phrygia and Thrace. Dionysus was a vegetation god, but one associated with trees and the vine, sap and wine, rather than cereals. There are many myths about celebrations of his festival by women who took to the mountains, where, in a trance-like state, they ate the raw flesh of animals. It is possible that the festivals did in fact provide rare occasions for women to leave their husbands

and their confinement to home and duty for a brief period and to take part in celebrations, which often seemed to involve dancing.

Ecstatic cults and those that emphasized the importance of the after-life were criticized in the Classical period. In a sense they looked forward to a different kind of religious sensibility that we perhaps recognize today. They were departures from the religion that was normally practised in public in Greece at this period.

Normally a cult was observed by acts rather than beliefs. The practice of worshipping a deity, bringing votive offerings to it, being present at a sacrifice, meant that the head of a household publicly displayed his membership of his community and culture. Festivals celebrated what was important to people: the events of the agricultural year, the founding of a city or a state, the death of a hero, the right order of society – including conflict between the sexes and rites of passage from one stage of life to the next. Gods had to be propitiated, given gifts in exchange for favours, so that they would withhold their potentially harmful powers and work on man's behalf. They could be asked for guidance and for healing. They loved beautiful things and noble deeds, and these things could be dedicated to them. It is clear that religion was a social cement and an occasion for pious observance, celebration and public demonstrations of right living.

The myths about the gods set down by Homer and Hesiod and other poets and prose writers were, then, inherited stories that had for a long time provid-

ed a way of talking about human experience through enjoyable narratives. They dealt with supernatural experience, human emotion and the functions of the natural world in a poetic way, through the use of metaphor and allegory. Once they were set out in writing and organized into a commonly accepted system of belief, the myths provided a pattern for this belief,

a succession of examples. It was natural, as time went on, that this system should be challenged.

Some commentators on the myths write about a change in Greek thinking from *mythos* to *logos* between the seventh and the fourth centuries BC, to suggest a move from mythical thinking to a more rational explanation of the world. This was, however, a very slow and complex process and one that probably did not affect most people in ancient times. It is interesting to note that one of our best sources for the myths is Apollodorus, who did not set them out until the second century AD, when they were clearly still popular. There were, however, a number of individuals who struggled to find alternative ways to think about the world and how it was formed.

Among the earliest were a group who lived in Miletus in Ionia on the west coast of Asia Minor (now Turkey) at various times in the fifth century BC. Throughout the seventh and sixth centuries BC there had been a coming together in Ionia of knowledge about other cultures and this had led to the realization that both Eastern and Greek myths of creation had certain features in common, so some men began to feel that the basis of their own beliefs was probably purely conventional and that they might therefore be questioned.

Between the end of the sixth century and the beginning of the fifth, Heraclitus began to talk about one central force that directed nature, an intelligence 'that does and does not want to be called Zeus'. Thus he removed himself to some extent from the habitual dependence on thinking by means of concrete examples. Gradually the importance of argument for its own sake asserted itself, as evidenced by Plato's fourth-century accounts of Socrates's fifth-century dialogues. Plato objected to the mythical gods and heroes on moral grounds, but in his powerful literary style he created something very like myths of his own to express those things that cannot be said in ordinary speech.

Perhaps the complexity of these matters is best illustrated by the opening of Herodotus's Histories, which he calls his 'Researches', and which are often based on his own careful observation. These were written some time in the fifth century, and he begins with accounts of how certain peoples came into conflict, quoting as examples the clearly mythical stories of the abductions of Io, Europa, Medea and Helen. He then dismisses these accounts with 'So much for what Persians and Phoenicians say ... I prefer to rely on my own knowledge'. So he passes on to what he perceives as a historical account of King Croesus of

Lydia, which actually sounds similarly mythical to us.

It is important to remember that the heroic world presented by Homer represented the historical truth to its original audience, that his heroes were their forbears, and his gods their gods. His poetic works were taught in school to the children of aristocrats, many of whom would be the future rulers and magistrates of cities. It is difficult to overestimate the influence of his works on the ancient Greeks. It is also difficult to exaggerate the richness, detail and interconnectedness of the myths by his period.

CHAPTER THREE
THE BIRTH OF THE GODS

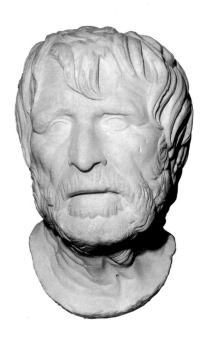

(British Museum)
Portrait bust of the poet Hesiod who wrote about the Creation of the Gods.

We are dependent upon writers who lived in or after the ninth or eighth centuries BC for our knowledge of ancient Greek myths and have to accept the fact that we cannot know who told these stories for the first time nor how they had changed over the centuries before the writers set them down. We can gain some idea of certain scenes and narrative events from the works of sculptors, engravers and painters, but we still have to refer such scenes back to written accounts to identify them with any certainty.

Surviving visual images and works of literature preserve comparatively few versions of the group of myths that concerns the beginning of things, the creation of the world and the gods. It is an unusual phenomenon, as in many cultures creation myths are both popular and important. The natural tendency of the Greeks seems to have been to shape their gods in as human and beautiful a form as possible, rather than in the inhuman or grotesque forms found in some other mythological systems. They also seemed indifferent to deities who were merely personifications of abstractions or of natural phenomena, and who did not make good stories.

Shortly after the heroic epics of Homer were written down in Ionia, a poet called Hesiod, from Boeotia on the mainland of Greece, wrote didactic epics, poems whose aim was to teach. One of these, written some time in the eighth century, is called Theogony, or the Creation of the Gods. It is actually also a cosmogony, for in it the poet recounts the story of the creation of the world as well as the birth of Zeus and 'the holy race of gods'. In this poem it seems likely that he collected up a number of myths on these subjects that were current in his day, some of them probably dating from centuries earlier and originating in different cultures; it is also likely that he made embellishments and additions of his own. Because it is the single most comprehensive text we have on the Greek creation myths, it is worth looking at it in some detail to provide an introduction to the subject.

Chaos was there at the beginning, says Hesiod; by Chaos he did not mean confusion but a kind of yawning void. Next came Gaia, or Ge (Earth), and Tartarus (a dark place below the earth) followed by Eros (Love). Then Night and Erebos (Darkness) came from Chaos; Night gave birth to Day and Ether (the air above us), having conceived them with Erebos through the power of Eros. After this, without the help of a mate, Earth produced Ouranos (Heaven) to be her equal and her comforter and to provide a home for the gods who would come later; then she gave birth to the mountains and the sea. She then mated with her self-created consort, Ouranos, and gave birth to Oceanus. The name Oceanus, or Ocean, did not imply the sea but the great river the Greeks imagined as perpetually eddying and circling round what they perceived as the flat disc of the known earth, and beyond which lay mysterious lands. From this union came other children also: Koios, Kreius, Iapetos, Hyperion, Theia, Rhea, Themis, Mnemosyne, Tethys, Phoebe and Kronos.

These children were known collectively as the

Titans and seem to be figures from an extremely remote past who feature very little in familiar Greek myths. The general view is that they perhaps represent distant memories of pre-Greek spirits of the natural forces exerted by the sky and the earth. Mnemosyne is, however, simply an abstract personification of Memory. We later discover that three males among the group of Titans – Kronos, Oceanus and Iapetos – mated with three females – Rhea, Tethys and Themis. Kronos and Rhea play an important part in later events.

Earth next gave birth to three monsters, the unpleasant but skilled and energetic Cyclopes, so-called because each had only one round eye set in the middle of his forehead, and to three unspeakable hundred-armed and fifty-headed sons, called Kottos, Gyes and Briareus. After this catalogue of births, the poem now springs into action. Ouranos hated the sons he and Gaia had created and hid them back inside her body. She suffered huge pangs as she

LEFT
(National Archaeological Museum, Athens) Bronze statue, 5th century BC, found in the sea off Cape Artemision, thought to be either Zeus holding his thunderbolt or Poseidon wielding his trident.

BELOW
Petra Tou Romiou: the rock on this shore in Cyprus marks the legendary birth place of the goddess Aphrodite when she rose from the sea. Her cult is thought to have arrived in Greece from Cyprus.

strained to eject them, and she devised a plan to free herself of the torment.

She shaped a mighty sickle and called upon her Titan sons to help her. The only one who volunteered was the youngest, Kronos. She hid Kronos, who waited until he saw Ouranos come to Gaia at night, stretching himself over and around her, in the way that Heaven always embraces Earth. At that moment Kronos moved; he cut off his father's genitals and threw them away from him. Drops of blood fell from them on to Earth and, as a result, a year later she gave birth to more children: the Erinyes (Furies), the Giants, and certain nymphs. Ouranos's severed genitals fell into the sea, where they floated for a long time, surrounded by white foam. From this foam emerged a beautiful girl who was carried on the foam first to Kythera and then to Cyprus, where she came to land. As she walked ashore grass sprang beneath her delicate feet. This was the goddess Aphrodite. Love and Desire followed her and became her constant companions.

Hesiod then gives the names of the children born to Night; some of them were simple abstrac-tions, but among them were the Hesperides and the Destinies. Pontus (the Sea) fathered Nereus, a sea-god, who has become most familiar to us as the father of the Nereids, or sea nymphs. Another of the sons produced by the Sea and the Earth later married the daughter of Ocean and fathered Iris, the goddess of the rainbow, and the Harpies, female winged crea-tures who appear in various guises in different myths. Hesiod associates them primarily with the force of the wind, but we shall find them behaving like evil and aggressive birds elsewhere.

According to Hesiod, two of the children of the Sea and Earth married and produced the sisters called the Graiai (Grey Ones) and also the Gorgons, one of whom, Medusa, was mortal.

When Perseus killed Medusa, in a myth that will be recounted later in this book, two creatures sprang from her: the flying horse, Pegasus, and Chrysaor. Pegasus later flew up to live with the gods on Olympus, but Chrysaor fathered some monsters: Geryon (later killed by Heracles) and Echidna, half-woman and half-snake. She in turn produced mon-sters familiar to us through myths: Cerberus (the

(Terme Museum, Rome) Relief showing the birth of Aphrodite, who is being helped from the sea by two nymphs, c.460 BC. The relief forms the front of the so-called 'Ludovisi throne' which may be part of an altar. It was the work of a Greek sculptor and was found in Rome.

37

hound of Hades), the Hydra of Lerna (another victim of Heracles), the Chimaera who had the heads of a lion, a goat and a snake (killed by Bellerophon), the Sphinx (defeated by Oedipus) and the Nemean lion (also subdued by Heracles). Scholars suppose that these creatures have their origins outside Greece and may be oriental. In Greek myths, as we shall see, some are associated with the underworld. Most of them are perceived as being dangerous foreign creatures, in the sense that they live outside the natural order of things and threaten peaceful society; heroes have to destroy them in order to restore normality. They may once have been deities in distant countries, but they have been incorporated into Greek mythology as grotesque monsters.

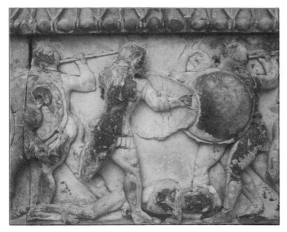

Hesiod next describes the children of Oceanus and his wife: they are all the rivers of the world and all the river nymphs, among them Styx, the river across which souls were ferried to the Underworld by Charon. Hesiod says Oceanus has so many roaring rivers among his sons that it is hard for mortal men to name them, 'but they are known to those who live nearby'. The phrase reminds us that all Greeks perceived their local streams and rivers as being sacred, however obscure they were.

The poem then describes the offspring of a number of the Titans, few of whom have an important place in popular mythology until we come to the children of the youngest son, Kronos, who forced a union with his sister Rhea. Their children were Hestia, Demeter, Hera, Hades, Poseidon and Zeus, who were to become major figures among the gods of Olympus. Kronos had learned from his parents, Ouranos and Gaia, that he would one day be overcome by one of his sons. Therefore, in a reversal of his father's action when he pushed his children back into their mother's womb Kronos swallowed each of his sons as he was born. Their mother, Rhea, suffered great grief, just as Gaia had suffered great physical pain. When Rhea was about to bring forth her last son, Zeus, she appealed to her parents, Ouranos and Gaia, to help her conceal the birth. They sent her to Crete, where Gaia agreed to nurture the child. When Zeus was born, at Lyktos on Crete, according to Hesiod, Rhea hid him appropriately, deep under the earth in a vast cave on Mount Aigaion. Meanwhile, Rhea took a giant stone, wrapped it in swaddling clothes and gave it to Kronos, who swallowed it down, assuming it was his last son.

The young Zeus grew quickly in strength and beauty. By some means Rhea persuaded Kronos to vomit up the children he had swallowed. The first to emerge was the stone, which had been swallowed last, and this was set at 'holy Pytho' (Delphi) in a cleft beneath Mount Parnassus, to be a wondrous

sign to men. Once his brothers had been freed from Kronos's stomach, Zeus returned and freed his uncles, the monster-like children of Ouranos, from the bonds with which Kronos, in envy of their strength, had earlier bound and imprisoned them. In binding the Cyclopes and the monsters, who were his brothers, Kronos had lost their allegiance forever.

War now broke out between the young gods and the Titans. The young gods based themselves on Mount Olympus and the Titans on Mount Othrys. The savage battle raged on for ten years; it blasted the earth with storms, earthquakes, floods and droughts. In an effort to end it, the Olympian gods fed the six monstrous brothers of Kronos with their own food of nectar and ambrosia and appealed to them for help. The Cyclopes, in gratitude for their freedom, gave Zeus the thunderbolt and lightning that became his characteristic weapons ever afterwards. Their three many-armed brothers used their strength to hurl huge rocks at the Titans. At last the Olympian gods and their allies defeated the Titans and imprisoned them in Tartarus, as far beneath the earth as heaven is above it.

In order to avenge the Titans, Gaia's brood of Giants revolted against the gods in another fierce struggle, known as the Gigantomachy, in which the mortal, Heracles, came to the help of the gods, who finally won the battle. Gaia then mated with Tartarus and, as her last child, bore mighty Typhoeus, a monster with a hundred dragon heads, which all breathed out fire so that the earth groaned and the sea boiled. Zeus attacked the monster with his thunderbolt and finally maimed and defeated him, hurling him down to Tartarus. This episode may, of course, recall memories of early, violent volcanic activity that certainly took place in the Aegean area.

As it can be seen, there are various puzzling inconsistencies in the story of the birth and succession of the gods and it is also uncharacteristically grotesque and savage. Many scholars suggest indeed that it includes stories from different cultures, and they find in the castration of Ouranos episode parallels with a Near-Eastern tale, extant in Hittite texts, but possibly spread by the Hurrites and originating in Babylon. Certain elements seem to come from nearer home. For example Gaia and Rhea, whose fertility is inexhaustible and who put care for their children above care for their husbands, seem to have a good deal in common with the female deities of Minoan Crete. Neither is it surprising to find that in this story

Zeus was born in a cave on a mountain in Crete, which was exactly the sort of place where cults had been practised since early times.

The Titans are difficult to explain since they figure so little in Greek mythology as a whole, apart from Kronos who ruled, in a myth at least as old as this one, over an innocent and happy golden age. The most common explanation is that they represent a poetic way of dealing with an earlier order of belief that gave way to a new one. The gods who defeated the Titans were the gods of current belief in Hesiod's day; in winning the war, they seized power, restructured belief and buried old ideas forever. The movement from one set of beliefs to another can be seen in action by the way in which the cult of Gaia, the earth goddess, gave way to that of Apollo, the Olympian god, at Delphi.

It is worth noting that Chaos, Gaia and Eros – the Void, the Earth and Love – were the first things to come into existence, and that there was no single divine principle that created everything. The gods who emerge as rulers in this story are, apart from Aphrodite, descended from Gaia, or the earth itself.

CHAPTER FOUR
THE GODS OF OLYMPUS

The Olympian gods make their presence felt throughout Greek literature. In the *Iliad* and the *Odyssey* Homer allows gods and goddesses to concern themselves with individual heroes and to favour one side rather than another in conflicts. More can be learnt about the gods from thirty-three poems that are known as Homeric Hymns or Preludes because they are written in a metre characteristic of Homer's epic verse, although they actually date from a number of different periods. The plays of the Classical period demonstrate the powerful influence of the gods on men and women, and there are accounts of the myths concerning the gods in a number of prose works dating from later than that.

Pictorial images of the gods alter with changes in contemporary artistic styles, but also in accordance with their varying popularity at different times and in different places. Some account will be given here of each of the Olympian gods, beginning with the greatest of them.

Mount Olympus, part of the highest mountain range in Greece, rising to 2917m (9570 ft), and the traditional home of the gods. It lies in the north of the country, on the borders of Thessaly and Macedonia.

ZEUS

Although the last-born of his brethren, he was always the first in importance. The root meaning of the early form of his name, Dies, (also found in Latin *dies* 'day'), is 'bright' or 'shining', and he was clearly associated with the sky. He parallels gods from other Indo-European speaking races, for example the Indian Dyaus and Roman Jupiter, who are also sky gods. Homer calls him 'father of gods and men', and this reflects the word pater, 'father', that is found in Sanskrit Dyaus-pitar.

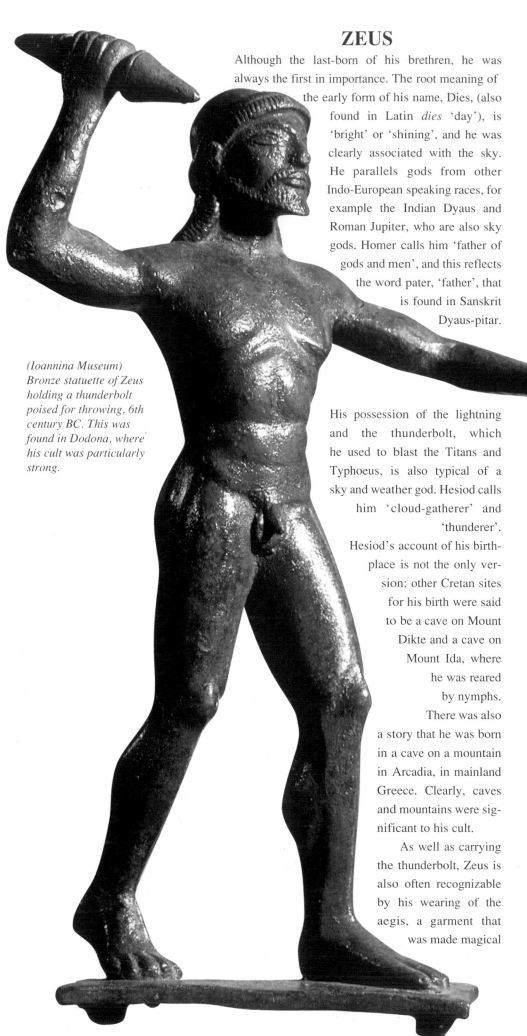

(Ioannina Museum)
Bronze statuette of Zeus holding a thunderbolt poised for throwing, 6th century BC. This was found in Dodona, where his cult was particularly strong.

His possession of the lightning and the thunderbolt, which he used to blast the Titans and Typhoeus, is also typical of a sky and weather god. Hesiod calls him 'cloud-gatherer' and 'thunderer'. Hesiod's account of his birthplace is not the only version: other Cretan sites for his birth were said to be a cave on Mount Dikte and a cave on Mount Ida, where he was reared by nymphs. There was also a story that he was born in a cave on a mountain in Arcadia, in mainland Greece. Clearly, caves and mountains were significant to his cult.

As well as carrying the thunderbolt, Zeus is also often recognizable by his wearing of the aegis, a garment that was made magical by his power. It is often shown as fringed, probably because it would originally have been a goat-skin, worn as a protection against bad weather, as they sometimes are by Greek shepherds today. The god often has an eagle with him, whose associations with the sky are obvious. The tree that was especially sacred to him was the oak, which once grew abundantly in Dodona where he was particularly worshipped, and which is, of all trees, most susceptible to lightning.

Once established as the chief of gods, Zeus lived in a palace on the highest peak of Olympus, as an early king would have lived on the summit of a hill. He was clearly conceived by people to whom rule by a king and a noble family was the natural order of things. He emerged from battle as permanent ruler of the world, since he was immortal, and he avoided the jealous fears of his predecessors by sharing his rule with his brothers and establishing his family around him.

Zeus and his brothers, Poseidon and Hades, agreed to hold Olympus and the earth in common, but cast lots for dominion over the sky, the sea and the underworld, dividing the three areas between themselves in a version of the system of inheritance we now know as partible that was common enough in antiquity, and indeed later. Zeus drew the sky as his portion, Poseidon the sea and Hades the underworld. For this reason, although Hades continued to be an immortal god, he seems never to have been thought of as an Olympian.

Zeus now turned his attention to women and to the extension of his family. The liaisons of the god are puzzling to us, and were objectionable to some people who worshipped him, because they break the normal customs of the time concerning monogamy and incest. It seems clear that they arose as a way of explaining two things. First, they brought the female deities of existing native cults into submission, or at least partnership, with the premier male deity of an invading people. Secondly, they are sometimes a purely allegorical way of explaining the god's acquisition of certain qualities. In any case, after a number of early marriages, Zeus settled down to a permanent marriage with one divine wife, straying thereafter to human mistresses in a manner that would have been found fairly normal and that will become clearer in the retelling of some of the myths.

The first wife chosen by Zeus was Metis, whose name means 'wisdom' or 'good advice'. He was advised that any son born of this union would over-

power him so, in an action reminiscent of his savage father, he swallowed his wife. Thus, allegorically, the god can be said to have swallowed wisdom, which was to be his innate quality thereafter. The story is more complex than that, however. Some time later Zeus suffered from a violent headache and Athena, his warrior daughter, sprang, fully armed, from his head. Vase-painters often illustrate this by showing Hephaestus assisting the birth by taking an axe to the head of Zeus. Here we can see the assimilation of an old cult to a new one. Athena seems to represent a goddess who had been worshipped in Greece at least since Mycenaean times and who therefore could not be born as a child from a newer god. By springing complete from her father's head, she remains herself and retains her importance, yet she is no longer supreme.

Zeus then married the Titan Themis, whose name means Custom or Law, and whose children were the Seasons and the Moirai (Fates). A similarly allegorical union with Eurynome, a daughter of Oceanus and Tethis, resulted in the birth of the Graces. He next married his powerful sister Demeter, an early divinity of grain and fruitfulness,

and their daughter was Kore, the Maiden, who is usually known as Persephone. The marriage of Zeus to Mnemosyne resulted in the birth of the nine Muses; thus the arts sprang from the union of divinity with memory. Two new Olympian gods resulted from Zeus's next union with the Titan Leto: the twins Artemis and Apollo became important members of the pantheon.

Finally, according to Hesiod, Zeus married Hera, who became his permanent, immortal wife. Homer, however, says that she was his first wife. She was also his sister, and in this and their marriage we may perhaps see a double attempt to rationalize the assimilation of the very powerful and well-established cult of Hera that had long been celebrated in the Argolid to the cult of the new chief god. Their children were Hebe and Eileithyia, representing youth and childbirth, and Ares, the rather blundering god of war. Without the help of any partner, Hera then gave birth to Hephaestus, the

god of metal-work and fine craftsmanship.

The Olympian pantheon now, therefore, consisted of Ouranos's daughter Aphrodite; Kronos's children: Hestia, Demeter, Hera, Hades, Poseidon and Zeus; Zeus's children: Athena, Artemis, Apollo, and Ares, and Hera's son Hephaestus. To these were later added Hermes, son of a liaison between Zeus and Maia (the daughter of Atlas, a Giant who had been sentenced eternally to support the earth on his shoulders), and Dionysus, the son of Semele, who is a mortal woman in Greek mythology, but was probably an adopted Phrygian earth-goddess. Busy, quiet Hestia, goddess of the hearth and home, seems gradually to have yielded her place in the ruling group to Dionysus. Hades remained in the Underworld but, with this exception, Zeus now had his complete family about him on Olympus.

Something should be said of the relationship between Zeus and humankind. It has already been seen that he was wise and that he controlled the weather, and thus the earth's fertility. He has an almost inexhaustible list of epithets, which suggest that he was perceived as being involved in every sphere of human activity. He was known, for example, as Zeus 'Polieus', that is 'of the city', and was thus the god of civic leaders as well as farmers. Above all, he was thought to rule with justice. When Greek thought began to move towards monotheism it moved towards his powerful figure as the principle god.

Nevertheless, Zeus had had problems with mankind. It is interesting that Hesiod, who relates these, does not say how mankind was created; men were simply present in his newly made world, although women were not. Among the children of Iapetos, the Titan, was Prometheus 'the foreseeing', who was permanently at odds with Zeus. There is a story, not told by Hesiod, that this demi-god made the first men out of clay figures, into which Athena breathed life. Zeus did not love the first men and, among other deprivations, took fire from them. Prometheus therefore stole fire from heaven and took it back to men in a dry fennel stalk. In doing this he angered Zeus once again.

A popular story, retold by Hesiod, explains that Prometheus had already angered Zeus by his decision about how a sacrificed animal should be shared between men and the gods. Having killed an ox, Prometheus butchered it, separating the meat from the bones and the fat. He parcelled up the bones and fat, reconstructing the animal by wrapping them in its skin; then he squeezed the meat into the animal's stomach and asked Zeus to choose between the two parcels. The god chose the attractive-looking bulky parcel, full of fat and bones, and was naturally angry. Most scholars think this tale is merely a comfortable rationalization of the fact that when the Greeks sacrificed an animal they were simply butchering it for food, and it made sense to offer the inedible parts to the gods, especially since the fat would send a savoury smell more speedily up to Olympus.

The creation of women formed part of Zeus's revenge for this action. He persuaded Hephaestus to form a female figure out of clay; she was dressed and given beauty, charm, guile and deceit by some of the other gods, and for this reason called Pandora, 'all gifts'. Zeus sent her to Prometheus's dull brother, who accepted her as a wife, despite warnings from Prometheus that he should accept nothing from the gods. From rash curiosity, she opened a closed and prohibited jar, and so set free its contents – all the evils and illnesses that have since plagued the human race; only Hope remained, under the lid of the jar. From Pandora descended women, who have ever

(Nicosia Museum) This early vase of the Mycenaean period, found in Cyprus, shows Zeus and Hera riding in a chariot, c.14th century BC.

since been a torment to men, says Hesiod. This episode led to the terrible punishment of Prometheus by Zeus, from which he was released by Heracles, as we shall see. Once again, it seems likely that the story actually shows Zeus assimilating the power of an ancient god into his family; Prometheus perhaps represents the traces of an ancient fire-god, who was superseded by the Olympian god Hephaestus.

When Prometheus's son, Deucalion, married Pyrrha, Zeus sent a flood to destroy the human race, but Prometheus advised his son to build a wooden ark, in which he and Pyrrha survived the nine-day inundation. Deucalion made a sacrifice to Zeus for saving them and, pleased by this, Zeus showed them how to repopulate the earth by casting stones behind them, which then became men and women. This is clearly also an imported story, coming from a Middle-Eastern culture in which floods were important to agriculture, but it establishes the power of Zeus over the human race.

45

RIGHT
(British Museum) Hades carries
Persephone off to his Underworld
kingdom. Painted vase, c.380 BC.

BELOW
Poseidon brandishes his trident
on this Greek coin from Paestum in
the Gulf of Salerno, Italy. Paestum
was originally called Poseidonia
by the Greek colonists who founded
it c.600 BC.

POSEIDON

The brother of Zeus, is much less clearly defined in myths. He was primarily a sea-god, but was also associated with fresh water. He is usually shown carrying a trident that he sometimes used to release springs of water from the earth. His blows could also bring earthquakes of the kind that are still experienced in the area. He is usually presented as a violent and unruly deity.

Most of his children were also strong and violent, the Cyclops Polyphemus being a good example. Poseidon's constant enmity to Odysseus, described by Homer int the *Odyssey*, resulted from the maiming of Polyphemus by the hero. Poseidon also held a long grudge against the Trojans because the king of Troy did not pay him, as promised, for the strong walls he built round the city, and in the *Iliad* Homer shows how Poseidon supported the Achaian (Greek) side in the Trojan war.

Poseidon was also associated with horses, and sometimes called Poseidon Hippios (Poseidon of the Horse). In Arcadia, where both he and Demeter were worshipped as horse-headed deities, presumably in memory of some very ancient cult, there was a local story that she turned herself into a mare to escape his advances, but he then became a stallion and overcame her. One of the results of this union was Arion, a wonderful horse.

Another local story relates to Attica, land which both Athena and Poseidon wanted to rule. They held a contest in Athens, the chief city: Poseidon struck the rock of the Acropolis with his trident and produced a salt spring. Athena produced a growing olive tree, however, and was judged the winner.

DEMETER

Was the corn-goddess and the mother of Persephone. We know her story from the Homeric Hymn to Demeter. Demeter took her young daughter to Sicily to protect her from the attentions of Hades, the god of the Underworld, who wanted her as his wife. One day while Persephone was in the fields gathering flowers her attention was caught by one that was rare and fine. As she picked it, the earth opened and Hades drove out from beneath it in his chariot. He seized the girl and carried her off to his gloomy kingdom. Demeter was inconsolable at her loss and sought through the world for her daughter. Because she was the goddess of cereals and grains, while she was absorbed in her unhappy search famine struck the earth. When the sun told her that he had seen the abduction she was furious with the other gods for what they had allowed to happen. During her wanderings, she passed some time at Eleusis, where she was received hospitably and in return taught the rites that later became famous there.

Finally, Hades and Demeter were reconciled, and Persephone returned to the earth, although she had to live in the Underworld, in the house of Hades, for a third of each year because she had eaten some pomegranate seeds during her captivity there. Demeter then revived the earth's fertility. She chose Triptolemos, a son of the royal house of Eleusis, to take seeds and the skills of growing corn to the

places on earth where men did not yet know them. The importance of the story lies in its theme of the rebirth that follows death, the natural sequence of the seasons for an agricultural people, but a theme that was taken up on a different level in the Eleusinian Mysteries.

HERA

The wife of Zeus, was also his sister. She was chiefly seen as a goddess of women, in the role of bride and wife rather than mother. Perhaps for this reason, the children Zeus had with her are the least impressive of the gods. Hera had important early cults of her own, notably in Argos, and her chief significance to humans lay in her government of marriage. A number of local marriage rites, some involving wedding processions, were gradually associated with her marriage to Zeus. The fertile nature of their union is suggested by Homer in the *Iliad* when, as they make love on Mount Gargaron, the earth breaks lavishly into flower-embellished grass beneath them.

Myths about Hera are chiefly tales of her jealous

hounding of the women to whom her husband made love. She was also a relentless enemy of some of his love-children, particularly Heracles. Her vindictiveness pursued the Trojan, Paris, after he chose Aphrodite, not her, as the most beautiful goddess and she acted against his people during the Trojan war.

Some examples of her jealousy against the women impregnated by Zeus must suffice. When Leto was expecting Artemis and Apollo, Hera pursued her so vengefully that no country dared to take her in, until she was given shelter on the island of Delos. When Semele was pregnant with Dionysus, after visits by Zeus during which he had concealed himself, Hera advised her to make Zeus swear to grant her any wish and then to ask him to appear before her. He was thus obliged to do so, but the power of his divine presence and the lightning that accompanied it burnt everything in the room to ashes, except for the embryonic Dionysus.

When Zeus turned the pregnant Io into a cow to escape Hera's attentions, Hera first tethered her under the watchful gaze of many-eyed Argos and, when she escaped, pursued her through the world. There is a story that when Io reached Egypt she regained her human shape in order to give birth and that she then became the Egyptian goddess Isis. Io had been Hera's priestess and her story perhaps conceals a primitive reason for Hera's usual association with the cow, and with the peacock, whose tail is many-eyed like Argos.

ATHENA

Was a virgin goddess, uninterested in love. Her probable Mycenaean past is reflected in her warrior qualities, and she is usually shown with a spear and an aegis in the form of a shield that bears the Gorgon's head given to her by Perseus. When she sprang from her father's head, holding her spear, Olympus shook and a loud shout arose from the earth.

She was particularly associated with the city of Athens but it is not known which took the name from the other. There is a myth that helps to explain the connection. Hephaestus struggled to make love to Athena, and as she resisted him his sperm fell to the ground and fertilized the earth. Nine months later Erichthonius was born. Athena put the baby in a lidded casket, and gave him to the daughters of King Kekrops of Athens to care for, telling then not to open it. Two of them did so, however, and threw themselves over the Acropolis in terror at the serpents they saw inside. Athena then brought him up on the Acropolis herself and when he was an adult he

ABOVE
(British Museum) An early terracotta goddess from the Argolid, possibly representing Hera, 6th century BC.

LEFT
The Heraion of Argos. From early times Hera was the most popular deity throughout the Argolid. Her sanctuary, set above the fertile plain of Argos, reveals complex ruins on different levels. The site was first occupied in prehistoric times.

49

(National Archaeological Museum, Athens) Athena Promachos, the goddess in her manifestation as a warrior champion. Bronze statuette from the Acropolis in Athens, her home, c.500 BC.

became the king of Athens. This is a kind of myth that was frequently constructed to give legitimacy to an immigrant people's right to claim a particular city or state as their own. Greek names containing the element *chthon* are used to suggest that people are autochthonus or native to the place, that they sprang from the earth. In vase-paintings Erichthonius is sometimes shown with a serpent's tail, again suggesting that he came from the earth itself.

Athena was worshipped in her city for her introduction of the olive tree in the contest with Poseidon that has already been described. She has other qualities that make her an appropriate goddess for city-dwellers. She was a craftswoman, who was particularly skilled at spinning and weaving, as she demonstrated in her spinning contest with Arachne, who was turned into a spider for her temerity in challenging the goddess. It is claimed that she invented the flute, but threw it aside in disgust when she saw how ugly she looked as she played it. She was also interested in making chariots and warships, and she is said to have had a hand in building the ship called the Argo for Jason. Her popularity among the skilled vase-painters and boat-builders of Classical Athens is not surprising.

Athena's familiar creature is the owl. She is described as wise and as moral and righteous. Homer often refers to her shining grey eyes. She is sometimes known as Pallas Athene. Some people think this might be a reference back to the palladion or shield-shaped goddess of the Mycenaeans, others see in it the ghost of the story of her accidental killing of her friend Pallas, with whom she was brought up. Neither of these may be the reason. She was also often described as Promachos (Champion). For the same reason as Hera, she favoured the Greeks in the Trojan war, but unlike Hera she was a friend to Heracles and dealt tenderly with Odysseus.

ARTEMIS

Was another virgin goddess, but of a very different kind. She was a young huntress who also defended wild game, particularly young creatures. Perhaps because of her interest in young things, women called upon her in childbirth. Her name is not Greek and, although she was Apollo's twin sister and born with him on Delos, they were not worshipped in the same places. Her connection with wild animals is reminiscent of the Cretan goddess, described in *Chapter Two*, in her manifestation as The Lady of the Animals.

She was attended by a number of young women who defended their virginity fiercely. Among them was Britomartis, who had a Cretan name and a Cretan story. It was said she was pursued by Minos and leaped off a cliff to avoid him, but was safely caught in some fishermen's nets and later went to live quietly in Aigina where she was worshipped as Aphaia, which means Invisible. Another follower of Artemis was Callisto, who was raped by Zeus who tricked her by disguising himself as Artemis. Artemis was so incensed when she noticed Callisto's pregnancy that, in spite of the girl's innocence, she turned her into a she-bear and sent her away.

These stories suggest that some of the followers of Artemis might once have been deities similar to Artemis herself. Anthropologists today see in her roaming band of young virgin followers indications of a rite of passage, when a group of girls of almost marriageable age live together for a time outside the constraints of normal society.

Artemis was implacable in the defence of her own honour, and of that of her family. Niobe, the

happy mother of many children, foolishly boasted of her superiority to Leto, whose only children were Artemis and Apollo. At this, Artemis and Apollo seized their arrows; Artemis killed all Niobe's daughters and Apollo all her sons. Niobe, whose tears would not cease, and who turned into a stone that still wept, has become a permanent image of maternal grief. Artemis was responsible for the death of some men too, notably Actaeon who, while he was hunting in the mountains, watched her and her nymphs as they bathed in a pool. She caused him to be torn to pieces by his own hounds.

She was much worshipped in wild, mountainous places and this accords with her untamed nature.

APHRODITE

The goddess of love, is by no means virginal. We have already recounted Hesiod's story of her birth, but there is another. In this version Zeus was married to Dione, whose name is the feminine form of Zeus, and Aphrodite was their daughter. Homer also describes her as the daughter of Zeus. It seems likely that

Hesiod was reflecting the way in which eastern myths were slowly adapted to Greek ways of thought, for Aphrodite seems certainly to be eastern in origin, entering Greece from the islands of Kythera and Cyprus, where her cult was particularly strong at Paphos. Scholars see in her parallels with Sumerian, Akkadian and Canaanite love goddesses.

In the way of powerful goddesses, she had a comparatively insignificant husband, the lame metal-working god Hephaestus, who probably also originated in the east. She fell in love, however, with Ares, the war god. Hephaestus, who was a cunning craftsman, contrived a strong and fine-meshed net with which he entrapped them in the act of love and displayed them to the other, laughing gods.

Another of her adulterous unions was with a mortal, Anchises, who was the cousin of Priam of Troy. The son she bore from this union was Aeneas, who grew up to become a hero and the leader of the Trojan people after their expulsion from Troy. He eventually founded another city, which was later claimed to be the precursor of Rome. It was quite usual for great heroes to have one divine parent.

The most powerful myth about Aphrodite probably followed her from the east and tells of her love for Adonis. This is thought to be a version of the eastern myth of the great mother and her divine lover, which was also probably current in Minoan Crete. The story begins when Aphrodite caused a young princess to fall in love with her father and deceived him into making love to her under cover of darkness. When he discovered what he had done and threatened to kill his daughter, the gods turned her into a tree called by her name, Myrrh. In time, a beautiful boy was born from the tree. He was named Adonis, and because he had no mother he was given a choice of guardian. He chose Aphrodite, but was allowed to spend only two thirds of the year with her, being sent to spend the remaining months with Persephone in the Underworld. Adonis was killed by a boar when he was hunting, and flowers sprang from his blood. His myth can be compared with the Babylonian story of Tammuz, who was also a god who disappeared for part of the year and whose reappearance coincided

with the return of fertility. The seasonal festival marking the coming of winter, when women mourned for the death of Adonis, continued in Greece into historical times.

APOLLO

Was one of the most important gods, and his qualities and characteristics continued to be developed by writers right through to Classical times, when they were particularly appreciated. He was the god of music and poetry and of all kinds of inspired arts. He had some ability to heal, having probably assimilated the role of an earlier healing deity. He was also sometimes an aggressive archer, particularly in concert with his sister, Artemis. He is usually shown with a lyre and a bow, and sometimes with the birds that were particularly associated with him – swans, kites, vultures, and the crows used by seers as omens. In late periods he was sometimes identified with the sun, but this is not part of his early mythology.

He was close to Zeus and because he knew his father's will he was highly regarded as a prophet. The playwright Aeschylus, in the *Eumenides*, makes him say: 'I never lie. In my role as prophet I have never made a statement concerning man, woman or city that was not prompted by Zeus.' That play also demonstrates his highly developed morality as he pleads for mercy rather than vengeance for Orestes, who is on trial before the gods.

The birth of Apollo and Artemis on the island of Delos has already been mentioned. That story may have originated in a desire to account for the otherwise surprising fact that the Ionian cities chose to meet regularly on that small, rocky island for the Panionian festival, and Apollo had an important sanctuary there. His most famous sanctuary was, however, the one at Delphi. The story goes that he went to Delphi shortly after his birth and there slew a female serpent called Python, the terrible guardian of the place, so that he could establish himself there. Since it seems likely that there had long been a shrine to an earth goddess there, her representation as a serpent, who comes from the earth, and Apollo's defeat of her both serve to explain how an early cult was ousted by a later one.

OPPOSITE
(Corinth Museum) Roman mosaic of Apollo. In later periods Apollo began to be given new attributes and to be assimilated with other gods. Here he is shown as a sun god, and the grapes in his hair suggest that he has assumed some of the attributes of Dionysus.

LEFT
(Delphi Museum) An Athenian white-ground dish, c.480 BC, found in Apollo's sanctuary at Delphi, shows a garlanded Apollo pouring a libation from a cup. He is attended by a raven, a bird used in making prophecies, and holds his lyre. Details of the lyre are in low relief and might once have been gilded.

The Terrace of the Lions, 7th century BC, on the Island of Delos, leading to the precinct of Leto, whose cult was observed on the island and who is said to have clung to a palm tree there as she gave birth to Apollo and Artemis. Delos is the smallest of the Cyclades but was once a religious centre of the Aegean. Its oracle was next in importance to that of Delphi, and there was a great temple to Apollo there.

He is usually represented as a beautiful young man. Like the other gods, he pursued mortal women, but the women often met disastrous fates. Daphne, fleeing from his advances, turned into the laurel tree that bears her name. Marpessa, given the choice between Apollo and an insignificant human husband, chose the latter because he would age along with her, unlike an immortal god, and so be less likely to leave her as her youth vanished. Apollo attempted to seduce Cassandra of Troy by teaching her the skills of prophecy, but when she still refused him he modified the gift, which he could not withdraw, by making sure that no one would ever believe her prophecies, in spite of their truth.

Apollo loved Koronis, another mortal, but she deceived him with a human lover. When a crow, which was then a white bird, told him of this, Apollo shot Koronis with his bow and, in grief at his loss, turned the crow black. This story had a good outcome, however, for Apollo saved the child Koronis was bearing, and sent him to the Centaur, Cheiron, to be brought up. Cheiron was the greatest and gentlest of the Centaurs, creatures who were half-man and half-horse, and he educated a number of famous heroes. He was very successful in teaching Apollo's child, Asclepius, the arts of healing. The success of Asclepius in bringing dying men back to life disturbed Zeus, who sent him down to Hades with a thunderbolt.

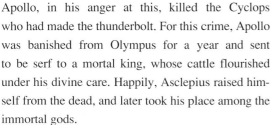

Apollo, in his anger at this, killed the Cyclops who had made the thunderbolt. For this crime, Apollo was banished from Olympus for a year and sent to be serf to a mortal king, whose cattle flourished under his divine care. Happily, Asclepius raised himself from the dead, and later took his place among the immortal gods.

When Apollo fell in love with Cyrene, he took her in a chariot to Africa, to the land that was named after her. There she gave birth to Aristaeus, who later became a deity of such rural occupations as bee-keeping, hunting and olive-growing. As well as other affairs with women, Apollo was also attracted to young men, such as Hyacinthus, whom he killed acci-

dentally with a discus, and who became the flower of that name. This incident might well represent the assimilation into Apollo's worship of an earlier young and beautiful god.

It was said that Apollo was a Hyperborean, that he came from a land beyond the north wind, and it seems likely that this deity actually arrived in Greece from the north. An annual ritual procession at Delphi always moved northwards, as though towards the land from which the god had come. It was said also that in the winter he handed the sanctuary over to Dionysus and withdrew to the blessed lands of the Hyperboreans, where the climate was always moderate, the crops good and the people just and happy.

(Epidauros Museum) Statue of Asclepius with a sacred serpent found at the sanctuary at Epidauros that was earlier sacred to his father, Apollo. As the healing cult of Asclepius grew more popular at Epidauros, he was said to have been born there.

HERMES

Was the younger brother of Apollo, and is usually shown by later artists as young. He often wears winged shoes, carries a golden staff and wears a hat, which is sometimes shown with the kind of broad brim that would keep the sun off a traveller's face. The Homeric Hymn to Hermes has a light tone, characteristic of this god. He was a native of Greece; his parents were Zeus and a nymph called Maia and he was both conceived and born in his mother's home, a cave on Mount Cyllene in Arcadia.

On the day of his birth he walked to the entrance of the cave, where he found a tortoise. He killed it and used its shell to construct a lyre, the first ever made. Then he took a long walk to Pieria, where he stole a herd of cattle that his brother, Apollo, was meant to be watching. Crafty Hermes made shoes for the feet of the cattle and drove them backwards to his cave, to confuse anyone looking for them. On the way home, he slaughtered two of them as a ritual sacrifice to the gods. He then returned to his cradle and played the part of an innocent baby.

In spite of his youth, he was summoned before Zeus, who ordered him to restore the cattle, which he did, together with Apollo's bow and quiver, which he had also appropriated. He soothed Apollo by giving him the lyre he had made, and in return Apollo gave him the golden staff he had used for driving cattle and also some lessons in minor divination. The incident is typical of Hermes, who did not share the moral grandeur of his brother, and who became patron of traders and thieves and all those who turn an honest or dishonest penny.

His chief function was to be herald, or messenger, to the gods. This task seems to have been based on his earlier experience as protector of travellers and god of roads and pathways. In his manifestation as Hermes Psychopompous, he also accompanied the dead to Hades. His name is similar to the Greek word used for heaps of stones that were used in the rocky country landscape to mark holy places and boundaries. He was a popular god, frequently worshipped, particularly by young athletes. At places of his worship people set up *herms*, simple pillars or stones that could be set up anywhere; these were often marked only by being topped by the representation of a human head and having male genitalia at an appropriate level.

Hermes is sometimes credited with fathering Pan, the rustic divinity, half-man and half-goat, who was the shepherd's god and who played the pipes, chased nymphs and grew ferociously bad-tempered if his afternoon rest was disturbed.

DIONYSUS

Was undoubtedly a foreign god. He was clearly felt to be a late arrival into the Pantheon, and may not have been absorbed into the system until sometime after 1000 BC. There are many myths about him, and the same myths have a variety of versions, as different writers and artists modified the narrative to suit their own purposes. Many of the myths concern the disasters that befell people who showed resistance to him or his cult, and it is possible that these reflect actual civic opposition to the spread of the cult, as well as individual doubts about the nature of the worship of Dionysus.

His birth has been touched on already. His mother was Semele, the daughter of Cadmus, King of Thebes, and his wife, Harmonia, who was the

ABOVE
(British Museum) Terracotta of Dionysus from Tanagra holding a cockerel and an egg, both symbols of rebirth, c.370 BC.

OPPOSITE
(National Archaeological Museum, Florence) Detail of the François Vase (called after its finder), painted by Kleitias in Athens (c.570 BC). It shows Hermes carrying the herald's staff and wearing his broad-brimmed traveller's hat.

daughter of a god. Semele's name is very close to that of a Phrygian earth goddess. It was in Thebes, however, that Semele was scorched to death by the visit from Zeus that Hera had persuaded her to request. Zeus took the embryo of his child from Semele's womb and stitched it into his thigh.

When Dionysus came to term and was born, Hermes took him to be nursed by Semele's sister, Ino, who was married to Athamas, King of Orchomenos. As a result of Hera's implacable pursuit of those who cared for her husband's love children, Athamas and Ino were driven mad; they killed their own children and Ino threw herself into the sea from a cliff-top. Dionysus was then given to the nymphs of Mount Nysa, who nursed him as a child and later became part of the group of followers who always accompanied him.

Once he had grown up, Dionysus somehow discovered the art of wine-making, which became one of his important attributes. This also enraged Hera, who sent him mad and caused him to wander for a long time through foreign lands such as Egypt, Syria and Phrygia. He was restored to sanity, some say by Rhea the mother goddess, who also taught him some of her mysteries. He then returned to Thrace.

This was the beginning of the god's travels through Greece and a number of hostile and violent encounters with his hosts. Euripides gives the most moving account of one of these in his play the *Bacchae*. When Dionysus returned to his birthplace, Thebes, the ageing former king Cadmus had given up his rule to his daughter Agaue's son, Pentheus. Pentheus was hostile to Dionysus and appalled by the behaviour of the women of his city, including his own mother and aunts, who left their homes and were 'gadding about' the slopes of Mount Cithaeron 'dancing in honour of this upstart god Dionysus.' Pretending to be a traveller, Dionysus advised Pentheus to disguise himself as a woman in order to see what they did on the mountain and put a stop to it. The women saw through the disguise and, in their wild frenzy, tore Pentheus apart. His mother Agaue lead the ferocious attack, and she did not discover the horror of what she had done until she recovered from her frenzy some time later and saw that the thing she was holding in her hands, which she had thought was a lion's head, was actually the head of her son. Euripides makes Cadmus reflect: 'If any man derides the unseen world, let him ponder the death of Pentheus, and believe in gods.'

When Dionysus arrived in Argos, the women wandered through the wild landscape and, in their possessed state, ate the flesh of their own children.

At Tiryns, the daughters of the king were hostile to the cult; they were punished by a frenzy which made them wander all over the mountainous country of the Peloponnese.

Dionysus also visited the islands and, in one version of a fairly common story about his sea journeys, he was captured by pirates. They found it impossible to keep him tied up, and the pilot of the ship realized that he was a god. The other men paid him no heed, however, and as the ship journeyed on, a vine grew from the mast, the ship ran with wine and their passenger turned into a lion. All except the pilot jumped over the side, where they were turned into dolphins.

Even the kindlier actions of the god resulted in distress. When he visited Attica, he was received with great kindness by a local ruler called Icarius. In return, Dionysus gave Icarius the gift of wine, which he shared with his people. When they felt the strange effects of this new drink, however, they imagined that they had been poisoned and killed Icarius, whose daughter then hanged herself for grief.

The cult spread, nevertheless, but its practices were clearly very different from normal civic, well-regulated processions and offerings made by the male heads of households. Something has already been said about the development of this cult in *Chapter Two*. The celebrants drank wine and, apparently, ate raw flesh in order to assimilate the god into themselves and they danced themselves into an ecstatic state. Dionysus is usually accompanied by a trail of women followers, the Bacchantes, together with a collection of obviously sexually active young satyrs, and usually at least one elderly, bloated, drink-sodden Silenus.

ARES

The god of war, is perhaps the least developed of the whole Pantheon, probably because Athena was a much more skilful fighter and he was, in a sense, unnecessary. Although a god, Ares was actually wounded on a number of occasions, by Heracles and by Diomedes. He is shown as crudely violent and not popular with the other gods, apart from Aphrodite. He had some affairs with mortal women, but most of his children were unpleasant and violent. He is usually shown dressed in armour and helmet, and carrying a shield, spear and sword.

HEPHAESTUS

Was the son only of Hera, according to Hesiod, but of Hera and Zeus according to Homer. This may suggest a reworking of the myth by Hesiod's day to account for the decreasing importance of this god.

(National Archaeological Museum, Florence) Detail from the François Vase, c.570 BC. Hephaestus rides to Olympus on a mule. Dionysus had made him drunk as the only way of persuading him to go home and free Hera from the throne in which he had imprisoned her. A Silenus, one of the drunken followers of Dionysus, follows him. Hephaestus's lameness is indicated by his feet that point in opposite directions.

He is connected with fire, with metals and metal-working, and he ruled over the volcanoes that were his workshops, where, it is said, the Cyclopes assisted him. It seems likely that he came originally from outside Greece, from Lemnos or one of the islands near it, for in early times Mediterranean people were better metal-workers than the Greeks.

His myths connect him with Lemnos because they say that on one occasion he crashed to land there and damaged his leg when he had been hurled from the heavens and spent a whole day falling through the air. Other writers say that he was congenitally lame, and history tells us that working at a forge was a more appropriate occupation than agriculture for lame men.

His skill was consummate. It was because of Hera that he had been thrown from Olympus and, in revenge, he constructed a wonderful throne for her, which closed about her when she sat on it. The gods could not free Hera, so Dionysus was sent to get Hephaestus drunk enough to be brought on a mule to release her. He also made the strong web that he used to trap his wife and Ares as they made love. It was he who constructed the first woman, Pandora, from clay, and he made the chains that fastened Prometheus to a rock in the Caucasus so that Zeus could punish him. Achilles' wonderful armour was also the work of Hephaestus and he used flame as a weapon in the Trojan war.

HESTIA

The sister of Zeus, has a name that means simply Holy Hearth. The hearth was the centre of the house or palace, providing heat, light and warm food. There are no myths about Hestia because she was a virgin aunt who stayed at home and looked after everyone else. Yet because her cult was a family cult it was important to ordinary people.

CHAPTER FIVE
THE HEROES

Just as different regions of Greece had their own cults, so they also had their own heroes, some of whom were claimed as ancestors of important regional families. The adventures of these heroes were gradually woven into a rich and complex pan-Hellenic pattern in which they entered one another's stories and made connections between ruling families; if a thread is pulled from one of these myths it unravels several others at the same time. The gods themselves participated in the lives of the heroes, sometimes even in their parentage in the case of the demi-gods who had one divine parent.

The areas from which the best-known of these myths spring are Argolis, the area once ruled from the great Mycenaean palaces; Boeotia, whose chief city was Thebes; Thessaly, further north, and later Attica, whose chief city was Athens. Myths about the tragic fate of the ruling families of Argolis and Thebes will be recounted in a later chapter, as will the exploits of the heroes of the Trojan war. Here we shall be concerned with those regional heroes whose parentage was sometimes ambiguous and who, as young men, were forced by circumstances to leave their homes and to go on quests that led them to encounters with dangerous, even monstrous, enemies. In the course of their adventures they discovered their true identity, and usually found a wife and even a kingdom.

Their stories were sufficiently interesting to become part of the common stock of Greek myths that would have been well known to everyone. Because of this shared cultural inheritance, there was no need for poets always to recount the myths in detail; they could simply refer to them to make a point. Vase-painters could conjure up a whole narrative by painting one scene from it. Similarly, after the Greeks had defeated a mighty Persian force, a sculptured *metope* was made for the Parthenon depicting the mythical battle between the Lapiths and the Centaurs; this celebrated the notion of victory by indigenous people over powerful intruders by alluding to a story that everyone would have recognized, without having to make a direct triumphal boast that might have offended the gods.

Myths were a way of talking about experience and of presenting a picture of the past, not as it actually had been but as a construct that could be shared as a reference point. They are enjoyable stories, but they can also be used to instruct, to explain why things are as they are and why society operates in the way that it does, to account for place names and give authority to the foundation of cities, to examine man's relationship with the gods and the results of his moral choices, and to explore the lengths to which heroic men can go – to the extent of having to cross the border between the living and the dead on some occasions.

The myths are set in the past, but not in any recognizable time. The heroes are part of a society that is ruled by kings, and they themselves are young warriors, although they have sometimes become kings by the end of their story. They belong in the period Hesiod describes as the fourth age of man. He sets out five ages of man: in the first a golden race lived in happy, healthy prosperity; in the second a silver race lived only until they were hidden away by Zeus as spirits of the Underworld because they injured each other and neglected the gods. In the third age a race of bronze lived, worse than the one before, great warriors who died by their own hands and went to Hades.

The fourth age is the one that concerns us. Then there was a race of god-like heroes. Some were killed in battle and lie beneath the earth, but others have been rewarded with a carefree life in the Blessed Isles. Hesiod laments that he lives in the fifth age, in a race of iron whose men praise the bad and despise the just and good. Our predecessors, who still had contact with the gods, established a world we have spoiled.

The myths about the heroes have certain narrative patterns that have made some people compare them with folk-tales, but they have proved capable of bearing more layers of interpretation at different periods than folk-tales have. Nevertheless, certain motifs recur in many of them: heroes are often unaware of their true parentage or are disappointed of an inheritance; they are given advice by an oracle that they misinterpret; they make rash boasts, are punished for impiety, go on quests, succeed in impossible tasks that were intended to kill them, defeat violent enemies through strength or trickery; they often win a wife as a reward, kill a loved one by accident, inherit a kingdom and so on. They all travel, and by that means they gather up other stories into their own. The stories of five heroes will be recounted here; they are Perseus, Bellerophon, Heracles, Theseus and Jason.

PERSEUS

Was the son of Zeus and a mortal woman and was conceived in a strange fashion. A king of Sparta, Akrisios, had only one child, a beautiful daughter called Danaë. He longed for a son, but when he consulted an oracle he was told that, although he would have no more children, his daughter would have a son who would kill him. To avoid this outcome, he locked his daughter away, some say in an underground chamber of bronze, others say in a tall tower. Yet in spite of her father's care, Zeus found his way into Danaë's room in the form of liquid gold, which poured into her lap, and from which she conceived Perseus.

Fearing the consequences for himself of the birth of a grandson, Akrisios put Danaë and the baby into a wooden chest, which he abandoned to the sea.

(British Museum) Battle of the Lapiths against the Centaurs (half man-half horse), who had invaded their territory, from a metope on the Temple of Bassae, 5th century BC.

They survived, however, and came to land on the island of Seriphos, where they were found by an honest fisherman called Dictys, who was the brother of Polydectes, king of the island. Dictys cared for them until Perseus was a young man. By that time Polydectes wanted Danaë for himself, and considered how to rid himself of Perseus, her young son and protector. When Perseus boasted that he could bring Polydectes the head of the Gorgon, Medusa, the king took him at his word and sent him to get it.

There were three Gorgons, of whom only Medusa was mortal. They were creatures with snaky hair, teeth like boars' tusks, bronze claws and golden wings. Anyone who looked directly into the face of a Gorgon was turned instantly to stone. They had three sisters called the Graiai, women who were born old and who shared one eye and one tooth between them. Athena and Hermes decided to help Perseus on his difficult quest, so they led him to the Graiai. Perseus held the sisters to ransom by stealing their eye and their tooth until they told him the way to some nymphs who could help him further. Perseus returned the eye and the tooth and went to the nymphs, who gave him three gifts: winged sandals that would enable him to fly, a helmet that would make him invisible and a pouch into which he should put the head of the Gorgon once he had cut it off. Hermes gave him a sharp knife.

Thus equipped, Perseus flew across the sea to find Medusa. When he arrived, Athena gave him a bronze shield that shone so brightly it acted as a mirror. The Gorgons were sleeping and Perseus approached Medusa, holding the shield before him so that he looked at her reflection, not her face, as he cut off her head. As soon as he had done it, two crea-

tures sprang from Medusa's body. One was Pegasus, a winged horse, whose seed had been placed in Medusa by Poseidon; the other was a monster called Chrysaor, who was to become the father of the three-headed monster Geryon whom Heracles later dispatched. Perseus saved himself by putting on his helmet of invisibility; then he took off over the sea in his winged sandals, carrying the Gorgon's head in the pouch he had been given.

As he flew over a lonely Ethiopian shore he saw a solitary young woman bound to a rock. He went to her help, and found that she was Andromeda, a princess of Ethiopia. She was there because her mother, Cassiopeia, had foolishly boasted that she was more beautiful than the Nereids, the sea-nymphs, and Poseidon had sent a sea-monster to punish the King and his people for his wife's impiety. The monster would ravage the country unless the king left his daughter tied up on the shore as a sacrifice to it. Perseus slew the monster and rescued Andromeda. The king then gave her to Perseus in marriage as a reward.

Perseus and Andromeda returned to Seriphos, where they found that his mother had had to take refuge with Dictys in order to escape the unwanted attentions of Polydectes. Perseus went to the king's palace, where he stood before the assembled court and, looking aside, held up the Gorgon's head. Polydectes and his companions were turned to stone and Perseus handed over the kingdom to Dictys. He later gave the Gorgon's head to Athena, who placed it on her shield.

On his return journey with his bride to Argos, his birth-place, Perseus stopped to take part in the athletic games at Larissa. Meanwhile, his grandfa-

ABOVE LEFT
(National Archaeological Museum, Palermo) Greek gold plaque showing a Gorgon in a typical running posture, from Sicily, 6th-7th century BC.

ABOVE
(Louvre Museum) Relief amphora from Boeotia, c.660 BC, shows Perseus beheading the Gorgon, Medusa, with the knife Hermes gave him; he wears his hat of invisibility and his magic sandals and carries a bag in which to put the head. Perseus turns his head away from Medusa in order to avoid being turned to stone. In this early representation, Medusa has the body of a horse, probably because her father was Poseidon and she would give birth to the winged horse, Pegasus, as she died.

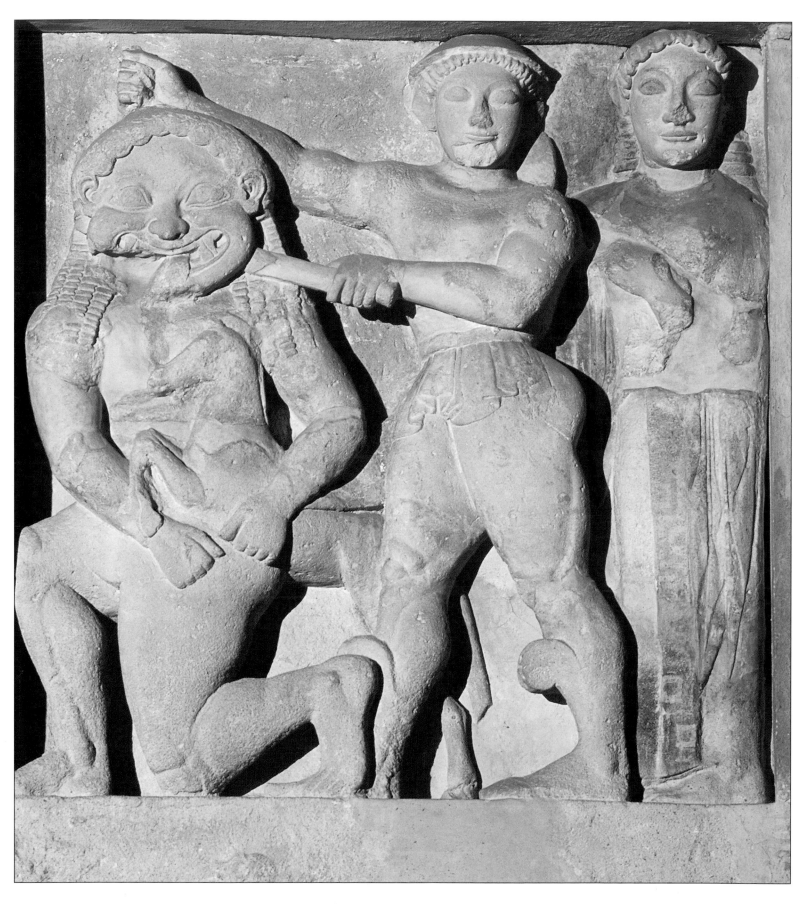

ABOVE
(National Archaeological Museum, Palermo) On this metope from a temple at Selinunte, Perseus beheads Medusa, who is holding the winged horse, Pegasus, to which she has just given birth. Athena, who assisted Perseus in the enterprise, stands by, c.530 BC.

OPPOSITE
(British Museum) Bellerophon, holding the reins of the winged horse, Pegasus, is here incised on an Etruscan cista, or cylindrical box, c.300 BC. When Greeks colonized parts of central Italy in the 8th century BC they had a profound influence on Etruscan art, which already benefited from rich resources of metal.

ther, King Akrisios of Argos, having heard that Perseus was returning home, fled from Argos, fearful of the prophecy that his grandson would kill him. Ironically, he too chose to go the games at Larissa, where the prophecy was fulfilled when a discus thrown by Perseus killed him accidentally. Perseus was so distressed that he could not bring himself to return to his newly-inherited kingdom of Argos, but exchanged it instead for Tiryns, which is why his descendants, including Heracles, ruled there.

BELLEROPHON

The myth of Bellerophon has similarities to that of Perseus, and tells more about the horse Pegasus. Bellerophon repeatedly dreamed that he was trying unsuccessfully to capture a wonderful winged horse. At last, Athena appeared in his dream, offering him a golden bridle. When he awoke he found he actually had the bridle in his hands so he went to the spring at Peirene, where he had seen the horse, and captured it with ease. The horse helped him to success in many of his later adventures.

Bellerophon lived for a time with King Proitos of Argos, until Proitos's wife tried to seduce him. When Bellerophon refused her, she claimed he had assaulted her, so Proitos sent him to Iobates, the king of Lydia, with a sealed letter instructing that the bearer of the letter should be killed. Iobates therefore sent Bellerophon to fight the Chimaera, a fierce, fire-breathing monster that was shaped like a lion, a dragon and a goat. Bellerophon succeeded in killing the Chimaera and Iobates gave him his daughter and half his kingdom.

After a number of other successful heroic expeditions, Bellerophon succumbed to pride, and tried to ride Pegasus to the gods on Olympus. The horse threw him to earth and went on alone. Bellerophon, injured in the fall, spent the rest of his life as a solitary wanderer, hated by gods and men.

HERACLES

(Hercules in Latin) is the most important of the adventuring heroes, and was probably the most popular of them in the ancient world. He seems to have originated at least as early as the Mycenaean period, and perhaps earlier, but additions were made to his story over the centuries. The incident of his assumption to Olympus as a god after his death might have been added in about the seventh century BC. He is a hero of conflicting qualities; he has the strength, appetites and unthinking brutality of wild nature and is subject to occasional fits of madness, but he can also show a desire to right wrongs and perpetuate civilized ideals. He had strong links with the

(British Museum) Bellerophon, mounted on Pegasus, kills the monster Chimaera, here shown as part-lion, part-goat. Terracotta relief from Melos, probably used as a hanging decoration, c.475-450 BC.

Centaurs, who were themselves ambiguous creatures, and he actually entered the Underworld yet came back to earth. To add to this, he was also sometimes the butt of jokes.

Heracles has local connections with both Argolis and Boeotia. He was born in Thebes in Boeotia, but his stepfather, Amphitryon, was actually a prince of Tiryns who was temporarily exiled in Thebes. The consummation of Amphitryon's marriage to his wife, Alcmena, was delayed until his return from an urgent military expedition. Zeus also admired Alcmena and, on the night of Amphitryon's return, disguised himself as her husband and lay with her first. When Amphitryon arrived, his suspicions were aroused by Alcmena's knowledge of his recent campaign, which she had gained from the disguised Zeus. He had his wife placed on a funeral pyre, but Zeus created a downpour to quench the flames, at

which Amphitryon understood and forgave her. As a result of the two unions, Alcmena had twin sons: Heracles, the son of Zeus, and Iphicles, the son of Amphitryon, who was nevertheless descended from Perseus and therefore, indirectly, from Zeus.

Zeus had unwisely prophesied that the next-born descendant of Perseus would rule over other leaders. Hearing this, Hera determined that it would not be Alcmena's son by Zeus. She therefore sent her daughter, Eileithyia, the goddess of childbirth, to delay the birth of Heracles and hasten the birth of another child who was descended from Perseus. This was Eurystheus, who was born at seven months. He grew up to be the king of Mycenae, whom Heracles later had to serve. Ironically, Hera's name is preserved in that of Heracles, which means Fame or Glory of Hera.

Heracles showed the great powers of a demi-god

as a baby when Hera, in her jealous rage, sent two enormous snakes to his cradle. Heracles woke up and strangled them both, thus also saving the life of his brother Iphicles. Iphicles' son, Iolas, became a devoted companion to Heracles on some of his later adventures.

When Heracles was eighteen he killed a fierce lion that was roaming on Mount Cithaeron. The ruler of the region gave him great hospitality in gratitude. Heracles is said to have slept with his fifty daughters either all in one night or on fifty consecutive nights. On his return journey to Thebes, Heracles met messengers from the King of Orchomenos who were coming to collect the tribute due to Orchomenos from Thebes. He cut off their noses and ears and tied them round their necks. In the ensuing retaliatory war, Thebes defeated Orchomenos and received tribute in its turn.

In gratitude for his valour during the war, the king of Thebes gave Heracles his daughter, Megara, as his wife. They had children and lived happily together until Hera, ever vengeful, struck him with a fit of madness that caused him to kill all his family. Polluted by this deed, Heracles had to leave Thebes, go to Mycenae and submit himself to King Eurystheus for twelve years. During this time Eurystheus gave him twelve labours or tests that he had to complete.

The Nemean Lion. His first task was to bring back the skin of the Nemean lion, a skin that could not be pierced by weapons. Heracles choked the lion in his strong arms, then used its own claws to skin it, and returned to the city with the skin slung across his shoulders. Because of this, he is usually shown wearing a lion skin as well as carrying a club.

The Hydra of Lerna. He was next sent to Lerna to destroy the Hydra, a many-headed water monster that lived in a swamp. It often ventured on to dry land and destroyed crops and animals in the surrounding region. Every time Heracles cut off one of its heads with his bronze knife, two new ones replaced it, and while he was struggling with it Hera sent a large crab to bite his legs. Eventually his nephew, Iolas, scorched the stumps with a flaming

(National Archaeological Museum, Athens) Heracles fights the Nemean Lion, the first of the twelve labours imposed upon him by Eurystheus.

torch as Heracles cut off the heads, until he had cut off the last head and buried it. Before he left, Heracles dipped his arrows in the bile of the Hydra so that they would inflict deadly wounds.

The Erymanthian Boar. Then he had to capture and bring back alive a huge boar that ranged over Mount Erymanthos and devastated local crops and herds. He travelled further from home on this quest and, as he was on his way to the mountain, he was offered hospitality by a Centaur called Pholos. Centaurs, who were four-legged creatures, with a man's head, shoulders, arms and torso and the long back and hindquarters of a horse, seem to have been either very rational, humane creatures, or very wild and vicious ones, rather as Heracles himself combined a desire to do right with wild and violent behaviour.

Pholos was sensitive enough to Heracles' needs to roast meat for him, although he ate it raw himself. He had a large jar of wine, which Heracles urged him to open. The other Centaurs were drawn to the wine by its smell and threatened violence to get it. After fighting them off, Heracles chased the survivors to Cape Malea, where they sought refuge with the great, humane Centaur, Cheiron, who lived there alone. In earlier times he had nurtured and educated Asclepius, Achilles, Aristaeus and Jason. As Heracles shot at the fleeing Centaurs, he accidentally wounded Cheiron with one of his poisoned arrows. Although he was immortal and could not die, Cheiron was in great pain and Heracles was able to release him from his suffering only by arranging that he should be allowed to go to Hades in exchange for Prometheus, which is another story.

Heracles continued his search for the boar, which he cornered in a snow-drift. He caught it in a noose, then tied it up and carried it on his shoulders to Eurystheus, who took refuge in a large bronze jar as soon as he saw it.

The Ceryneian Hind. This was a marvellous creature, sacred to Artemis according to some sources, that had golden antlers. It moved swiftly and Heracles spent a year pursuing it until he caught it in Arcadia when it was exhausted. After some pleading, Artemis allowed him to take it back as proof to Eurystheus before setting it free again.

The Stymphalian Birds. Heracles had next to destroy some birds that were increasing in number on the shores of Lake Stymphalos, between Mycenae and Arcadia. They are sometimes said to have had metal feathers and claws, and they fed on animals and men. He found it difficult to shoot them while they were roosting in the trees but Athena, who unlike Hera was sympathetic to him, gave him a bronze rattle made by Hephaestus. The noise of the

rattle startled the birds into flight and Heracles shot them down as they rose from the trees.

The Augeian Stables. Heracles had to clean the stables, or possibly the cowsheds, of King Augeias of all the dung that had accumulated there over many years; the king agreed to reward him with one tenth of all his herds if he completed the task in one day, knowing it to be impossible. Thereupon, Heracles diverted two rivers and channelled them together in such a way that they flooded through the stables and cleaned them out in one day. Augeias refused his reward, however, and in a later expedition Heracles killed him. Some people think this story was told to account for the great drainage dykes that had been dug in earlier times in the Peloponnese, which later inhabitants thought only a man of superhuman strength could have made.

To undertake the next three labours Heracles was forced to go further afield, away from his native Peloponnese.

The Cretan Bull. A mad bull was loose on Crete and Heracles had to capture it and bring it back to Eurystheus. A number of earlier stories have become involved with this one, and they give the bull different identities: some versions say it was the bull that brought Europa to Crete; others that it was the bull loved by Pasiphaë, the wife of Minos and mother of the Minotaur, that had originally been sent from the sea by Poseidon for Minos to sacrifice. Minos had incurred Poseidon's anger by substituting an inferior bull for the sacrifice so Poseidon caused the bull to become ferocious and a menace to the islanders.

Heracles captured it nevertheless and brought it home. When Eurystheus prepared to sacrifice it to Hera, she refused it because Heracles had brought it, so it was turned loose and wandered off to the plain of Marathon, where it later became part of the story of Theseus.

The Horses of Diomedes. Heracles had to go far northwards to Thrace to capture the horses of King Diomedes, which the king fed on human flesh. There are at least two versions of this story; the most com-

mon one tells how Heracles slew Diomedes, fed his flesh to the horses, then drove them back to Mycenae.

The Girdle of the Amazon. It is not clear whether this was actually a girdle or a piece of bronze waist armour, but it belonged to Hippolyta, the Queen of the Amazons – a race of female warriors, and she had received it from her father for bravery. The daughter of Eurystheus longed to have it, so Heracles was sent to the shores of the Black Sea to get it. He

(National Archaeological Museum, Palermo) A metope from a temple at Selinunte shows Heracles fighting an Amazon, a female warrior, c.5th century BC. While she holds an axe, he fights like a wrestler, holding down her foot with his. The limestone figures have eroded more than the marble heads.

(Villa Giulia, Rome) On this vase, Heracles, wearing the skin of the Nemean lion and carrying his club, brings the three-headed dog Cerberus to King Eurystheus from its home at the entrance to the Underworld. Eurystheus takes refuge fearfully in a large storage jar.

brought the girdle back, but accounts differ as to whether or not he had to kill Hippolyta to do so. Some say she gave it to him, others that Hera stirred up a war between the Amazons and Heracles' followers, in which the Queen was killed.

Heracles now had to go to the western edges of the known world, and even to the Underworld itself. **The Cattle of Geryon.** Geryon, or Geryones, was a

giant who had three heads and shoulders all growing from one trunk. He therefore had six arms, all of which held weapons. Heracles was sent to get his herd of cattle, which grazed in the far West, beyond the river Oceanus. First, Heracles had to kill a guard dog, Orthus, with his club; then he killed the herdsman and finally shot Geryon with his arrows. His chief problem then was how to get the cattle home,

and there are a number of tales about this. In one, he borrowed the cup that Helios, the Sun, used as a craft on the River Oceanus to make his return journey each night from west to east; in this Heracles transported the cattle across the river.

He then had a number of adventures on his way home, pausing to set up the Pillars of Heracles in the Straits of Gibraltar. His homeward adventures took place in what we now call France, Sicily and Italy, and the stories of these adventures became popular with the Greek colonists who had settled in those areas and who were thus able to identify the hero with their own localities.

Cerberus. Heracles was told to bring the dog Cerberus up to earth from Hades. Cerberus had been set in the Underworld precisely to guard it against

(National Archaeological Museum, Athens) Atlas brings the golden apples that he has picked in the garden of the Hesperides to Heracles, who has meanwhile taken his place in holding up the sky on his shoulders. White-ground vase.

intruders not just to stop people escaping; he had
three dogs' heads, a mane of snakes' heads and a
serpent's tail. So dangerous was the task of capturing
him, that Zeus sent Athena and Hermes to accompany Heracles.

While he was in the kingdom of Hades, Heracles
rescued Theseus, who had been sent there for trying
to help a friend capture Persephone and marry her
himself. Heracles then found himself moved to tears
by the story told by Meleagros, who had died recently, and he set Meleagros' mind at rest by promising to
marry his unprotected sister, Deianeira, on his return
to earth. He overcame Cerberus by squeezing him
round the neck. When he presented the hound to

Eurystheus, the terrified king told him to return it to
Hades immediately.

The Golden Apples of the Hesperides. Heracles
was next sent to gather golden apples from a tree that
was guarded by the Hesperides, nymphs who cared
for the garden of the gods on the western edge of
the world. The apples grew there on a tree that
Gaia, the Earth, had given Zeus and Hera as a
wedding present.

A number of stories are told about Heracles'
adventures on his journey to the distant garden. In
Libya he had to fight the giant Antaeus, who challenged, and defeated, all visitors. Heracles realized
that because Antaeus was a son of Gaia he drew his

strength directly from contact with the earth so he overcame him by lifting the giant up so that his strength evaporated. In Egypt he had to kill King Busiris and his son, who had intended to sacrifice him to Zeus. While he was in the Caucasus he found Prometheus, whom Zeus had chained to a rock in order to punish him for his impiety. Each day an eagle devoured his liver; each night a new one grew. Heracles killed the bird and freed Prometheus from his torment.

Prometheus then told him that no mortal could enter the garden of the Hesperides. Heracles therefore persuaded the Giant, Atlas, to go and collect the apples for him, while he relieved him of his perpetu-

al task of holding the heavens on his shoulders. When Atlas returned with the apples, it took all Heracles' ingenuity to persuade him to take up his burden again. Eurystheus feared to keep the golden apples that belonged to Hera, so Heracles gave them to Athena who had helped him.

After this, Heracles was free, but his life was no more straightforward. He won Iole, the daughter of a king, by beating her father at an archery contest, but lost her when he murdered her brother who was staying at Tiryns as his guest. This act broke all the sacred laws of hospitality, and Heracles was once more polluted.

He went to consult the oracle at Delphi, but was

(National Archaeological Museum, Palermo) Metope from a Temple at Selinunte, early 6th century BC, shows a simple representation of Heracles' punishment of the Cercopes, who nevertheless laughed at his hairy bottom which they could see while they were hanging upside down from a yoke over his shoulders.

refused advice, so he angrily wrestled with Apollo himself for the tripod. Zeus separated his two sons with a thunderbolt and then forced Heracles to sell himself as a slave for a number of years. He was bought by Queen Omphale of the Lydians, and there are stories of how they sometimes exchanged both their roles and their clothes.

During further travels, probably after his release from Omphale, he captured the Cercopes, two notorious criminals and murderers. He slung them upside down from a yoke across his shoulders, from which point they could see his hairy bottom, about which

they made so many jokes that he laughed and let them go. But he slew the owner of a vineyard who used to force strangers to dig his vineyard and then murder them.

Heracles took part in many military expeditions, which are too numerous to detail here. During this period he married Deianeira, as he had promised her brother he would, and stayed with her father for a time. After he had again accidentally killed a man, this time one of her father's kinsmen, he and his wife went into voluntary exile. During their travels they came to a river and Heracles asked the ferryman, who was the Centaur, Nessus, to take his wife across. Her screams alerted him to Nessus' assault on her, and he killed the Centaur by shooting a poisoned arrow into his heart. The dying Nessus, in apparent remorse, told Deianeira to mix his spilt sperm with the blood from his wound and to keep the liquid as a love philtre in case Heracles ever fell in love with another woman.

Later, Heracles went on an expedition against the king whose daughter, Iole, he had formerly won and lost. He defeated the king and returned with Iole. When Deianeira heard of his imminent arrival with another woman, she anxiously prepared fresh clothes for him, and dipped his tunic into the love philtre that she had taken from Nessus. She did not realize that because Nessus had been killed by one of Heracles' poisoned arrows, the philtre itself was a corrosive poison. When Heracles put on the tunic, it clung to his body and began to sear his flesh agonizingly.

He asked for a pyre to be made, then mounted it and persuaded a shepherd to set light to it. As the flames licked through the pyre, a cloud descended, caught up the hero and carried him to Olympus. Once there, he was reconciled with Hera, and given her youthful daughter Hebe as a bride. The gods then granted him the gift of immortality.

Further myths explain in great detail how the descendants of Heracles – the Heracleidai – came to rule over the Peloponnese, so that later rulers were descended from him. His three great-great-grandsons divided the area between them. In a later generation two brothers shared the rule of Sparta, which explained why Sparta had two kings down to historical times.

THESEUS

Is an Athenian hero, more polished than Heracles, but strongly associated with him in some of his exploits. Parts of his story must be very old, as they are set in a period when Athens was subservient to Knossos in Crete, but it seems clear that in sixth-century Athens his adventures were deliberately retold and extended both to emphasize their parallels with the popular Heracles and to give them a political dimension, making him responsible for acts that led to the foundation of Athenian democracy.

Theseus was conceived when Aegeus, king of Attica, who had no children, was visiting Troezen and made love to Aethra, the daughter of his host. It is said that the god Poseidon also made love to her on the same night. Before Aegeus returned to Athens, he left a sword and a pair of sandals under

(Argos Museum) Theseus fights the Minotaur, a man with a bull's head, in the labyrinth at Knossos in Crete. Vase painting by Hermonax, 5th century BC.

a heavy stone. He told Aethra that when her coming child was strong enough to lift the stone and claim these things, he should go to Athens and reveal himself to his father – until that time Aegeus feared that his ambitious nephews might harm the child.

In due course Theseus lifted the stone and claimed his birthright. He chose to take the hazardous inland route to Athens because he wanted to test his courage against the dangerous men and creatures who had begun to infest the land once again while Heracles was away serving Omphale.

First he dispatched the club-carrying brigand Periphetes, and took the club for his own weapon. Next he used the method of a murderer called Sinis on the murderer himself: he tied him between two pine trees that he had bent to the ground then released the trees; as they sprang up they tore Sinis apart. He then hunted and killed the notorious grey sow of Crommyon. On a narrow coastal path he met Skiron, who compelled those who wanted to pass to wash his feet, then kicked them over the rocks to a giant turtle that waited below. Theseus succeeded in tipping Skiron over the cliff. Nearing Athens he dealt with Procrustes, who offered travellers a large or a small bed, then stretched or shortened the travellers to fit the bed. Theseus killed Procrustes by fitting him to one of his own beds.

When the hero arrived in Athens he found that Aegeus was now married to Medea, the sorceress, who had convinced him she would bear him sons. She secretly divined the identity of Theseus, and wished to be rid of him, so she persuaded Aegeus that this strong newcomer might be dangerous and that he should be sent to Marathon to kill the ferocious bull that Heracles had driven from Crete. Theseus achieved that feat.

On his return a celebratory feast was prepared, at which Medea persuaded Aegeus to set poisoned wine for him. Before drinking, Theseus took out his father's sword to carve his meat. Aegeus saw it and recognized his son. He embraced him with joy, sweeping the poisoned cup aside. Medea was banished from the kingdom and Theseus overcame the nephews of Aegeus who had been a threat to his rule.

Theseus had arrived in Athens at the tragic moment when the city's tribute to Crete was due. Minos, the king of Crete, had never forgiven Athens for the fact that his son, Androgeos, had been murdered there. In compensation, he demanded a savage tribute: every three years, seven young men and seven young women had to be sent from Athens to Crete to enter the labyrinth and serve as food for the Minotaur who lived there.

The labyrinth, whose name possibly has some connection with the *labrys*, or double-axe symbol of Minoan civilization, may represent memories of the great, complex palace of Knossos. The myth says that the labyrinth was a dark maze of confusing passages, at the heart of which lived the Minotaur, a monstrous man with a bull's head. The maze had been designed by Daedalus. He had also designed the hollow bronze cow in which Pasiphaë, the wife of Minos, disguised herself in order to mate with the bull for which she had conceived a passion. The Minotaur was the result of that union.

Theseus pleaded to go to Crete as one of the victims, although they were normally chosen by lot. The ship set off, rigged with black sails, and Theseus promised his father to change the sails to white ones if he and the other victims returned home alive. On his arrival in Crete, Theseus met Ariadne, the king's daughter, who fell in love with him. In return for his promise of marriage, she gave him a ball, or clue, of thread to help him find his way out of the labyrinth.

As the Athenians entered the labyrinth, Theseus secretly fastened one end of the thread to the door, then he paid it out behind him as he moved towards the centre where the monster lurked. Once there, Theseus struggled long and hard with the Minotaur and killed him at last. Then he followed the thread back to the door and made for the boat with Ariadne and his fellow victims.

They sailed to Naxos where, for some reason, Theseus abandoned Ariadne, who was later discovered there by Dionysus. The usual version of the story is that the gods made Theseus forget Ariadne and sail on without her. Either in his joy at returning home, or in grief at the realization that he had lost Ariadne, Theseus forgot to change the black sails of his ship to white ones. Aegeus, waiting on the cliffs for the boat's return, saw the black sails and threw himself to his death.

Theseus succeeded to the kingdom of Attica and took steps to reorganize it. His most notable achievement was the unification of the small rural communities of Attica under the political rule of Athens, which made possible the future development towards democracy there. He continued to have adventures, however, including an expedition against the Amazons that parallels the one Heracles undertook. He also helped his friend Peirithous, King of the Lapiths, to defeat the Centaurs in the famous battle that broke out when the Centaurs invaded the Lapiths' territory during the King's wedding.

On two occasions he and Peirithous rashly

abducted the daughter of a god. They seized Helen when she was only twelve years old, and she was rescued by her brothers. Later, Peirithous conceived a desire for Persephone and Theseus helped him abduct her from Hades. For this, they were both confined to the Underworld, from which Theseus alone was rescued by Heracles.

When he was old, Theseus was displaced from ruling Athens. He took refuge in Skyros, where he died when the king, his host, treacherously threw him from a cliff-top.

JASON

Came from Thessaly. His father, Aison, who was King of Iolchos there, was driven out by his half-brother Pelias. Jason's mother, fearing for his safety, took him to the Centaur, Cheiron, to be brought up. The usurper, Pelias, consulted an oracle about his future and was told to 'beware a man wearing one sandal'. He was very concerned therefore on the day when a young man arrived at Iolchos wearing only one sandal, having lost the other as he helped a traveller across a flooded river. He was even more concerned when he discovered that the young man was his nephew, Jason. In the way of jealous kings, he sent Jason on a mission that he assumed would cause his death – the recovery of the Golden Fleece from Colchis at the far end of the Black Sea in Asia Minor, where it hung on a tree, guarded by serpents, in a grove sacred to the gods.

The fleece has its own story. King Athamas of Orchomenos, who was incidentally Jason's grandfather, had married Nephele, by whom he had a boy called Phrixos and a girl called Helle. He then took a second wife, Ino, who was jealous of her stepchildren. One year she encouraged the women of the kingdom to roast their grain before sowing it. Naturally there was no harvest, and Ino persuaded messengers who had been sent for advice to the Delphic oracle to return with the answer that the land would not be fruitful again until Phrixos and Helle were sacrificed. Preparations were made and, just as the children were about to be sacrificed, their mother, Nephele, came to the altar leading a sacrificial golden ram that had been sent to her by Hermes. The children clambered on to its back and it flew off towards Asia. Sadly, Helle fell from its back into the sea at a place that was named the Hellespont in her memory. The ram carried Phrixos safely to Colchis, however, where it was duly sacrificed to Zeus and its precious fleece hung in the sacred grove.

Jason accepted the challenge to travel to Colchis to bring back the Golden Fleece. Both Athena and Hera helped the craftsman, Argos, to build a good ship in record time. Athena brought oak for its prow from a tree sacred to Zeus at Dodona; this had the power of speech and was able to advise the crew. Fifty heroes eagerly joined the expedition. They were called the Argonauts but their identities vary in different versions of the story because many people later wanted to have an

(National Archaeological Museum, Athens) Ivory relief of a warship, from Sparta, late 7th century BC.

ANTIMAXO

(National Archaeological Museum, Florence) Detail of the François Vase painted in Athens by Kleitias, c.570 BC. It shows a ship that has come to pick up Theseus and the other young Athenians he has rescued from the Minotaur. One sailor swims ashore, eager to join in the dance of victory that has already begun.

Argonaut hero among their forbears. In the crew were certainly Argos, the boat-builder, the fathers of two of the heroes of Troy – Achilles and Ajax, Heracles, who seems to have been a late addition to the story, and Jason himself.

The crew made their first landfall at Lemnos, where they were delayed for a year by the women of the island who all needed new husbands, having recently killed their existing ones because of their misdeeds. The Argonauts finally dragged themselves away, but they had many other adventures on their way to Colchis, after one of which they were forced to abandon Heracles. In Thrace, they came upon the blind soothsayer, Phineus, who was starving to death

because every time he began to eat, the terrible winged women called the Harpies swooped down and either carried his food away or excreted foully on what was left. Two of the crew, who were sons of Boreas, the North Wind, flew after the Harpies, driving them on until they promised not to plague Phineus any more.

Phineus told the crew how to deal with their next hazard, the terrible Symplegades Rocks that clashed together. Jason took his advice and sent a dove between the rocks to test them. It emerged with only one tail feather missing, so the sailors made all speed between the rocks themselves, and found that only the stern of the Argo was slightly damaged.

At last they disembarked near Colchis and Jason went to meet the King, Aietes, and to plead for the return of the Golden Fleece. Aietes agreed, but first gave Jason a trial. He told him to yoke up two fire-breathing brazen bulls, the gift of Hephaestus, and use them to plough some land, which he must then sow with the teeth of the serpent that another hero, Cadmus, had killed.

Medea, the daughter of Aietes, was enchanted by Aphrodite into falling in love with Jason. She was a sorceress, like her aunt Circe, and gave Jason a magic ointment that would protect him and his armour against fire and weapons for a day. He smeared this on and managed to yoke the bulls and plough the field. When he had sown the dragon's teeth, hundreds of armed men sprang from the soil. He threw a stone among them so that they turned on each other and fought until they were all dead.

Medea, knowing that her father would never give up the Golden Fleece, guided Jason to the sacred grove and provided him with a drug that tamed the serpent. Jason lifted the Golden Fleece from the tree; then he and his crew, together with Medea and Medea's young brother, Apsyrtos, hurried to the ship and cast off as soon as they could.

Aietes pursued the ship, but the ruthless Medea killed her brother and dismembered his body, scattering it into the sea in pieces so that Aietes was forced to gather up the body slowly for burial. Zeus, in his anger at this impious murder, stirred up

a storm. Jason and the crew therefore put into Circe's island for ritual purification.

The Argo took a long and wandering route home, during which the crew had further adventures. When they arrived at Iolchos, they handed the fleece to Pelias and carried the Argo to the sanctuary of Poseidon. Medea decided to remove Pelias, the usurping king. She demonstrated to his daughters a method she had of revitalizing an old, sick ram: she cut it up and boiled it in a cauldron with certain herbs, until it emerged as a healthy young lamb; she suggested that the same treatment would rejuvenate their ageing father. Pelias, of course, died from the treatment.

Medea and Jason went to Corinth where they lived for many years, bringing up their children. Then Jason decided to take a new young bride called Glauke, who was the daughter of Creon, a local king. Medea prepared a robe for her, which she smeared with a terrible poison that seared the flesh of Glauke and also of her father when he tried to rescue her. Medea flew away from Corinth in a chariot pulled by dragons. As her final revenge on Jason, she killed their children. Then she went on to Athens where she married Aegeus, the father of Theseus.

Jason continued to rule in Corinth until the day when, as he sat peacefully near the Argo, in the spot where he had dedicated it to Poseidon, a timber from it fell on him and killed him.

OPPOSITE
(Vatican Museum) Attic relief, 5th century BC. The enchantress Medea instructs the daughters of the usurper, King Pelias, how to prepare a cauldron with boiling water and herbs to 'rejuvenate' their father.

CHAPTER SIX
THE TROJAN WAR AND THE RETURN OF ODYSSEUS

No one knows whether or not the Trojan War actually took place. When the archaeologist Schliemann, guided by Homeric evidence and his own instinct, discovered the remains of an important ancient city at Hissarlik, near the Dardanelles in north-west Turkey, he identified the city with Troy. Most archaeologists now think that the city he uncovered was too early to have been the one besieged in the Trojan War. All we can say is that there probably was an expedition to Troy from the Greek mainland in about 1200 BC, a time when evidence suggests that the weakening of the Hittite kingdom might have tempted invaders to attack some of its towns. Warriors from Greece might have mounted an important expedition to Asia Minor then with the intention of settling on the north-west coast, which had so far resisted them. It seems likely that they besieged and captured a number of towns, among which might have been a later, less magnificent Troy than the one Schliemann found, but that they returned home because they could not overcome the whole area.

Whatever the truth, for the Greeks the war against Troy was an established fact of their heroic past, and for that reason ought perhaps to be treated as legend rather than myth. Between the Mycenaean period and the writing down of Homer's poems in the eighth century, tales of that and other wars and the memorable feats of particular warrior heroes had clearly been repeated, elaborated and linked together as part of the material of the adventure to Troy. The heroes were named, and their names, together with

those of their ancestors and their homes, were repeated by singers or story-tellers in rhythmic lists and catalogues that made them easy to remember. In this way they became historicized.

Their feats may have been inspired by memories of the warrior Mycenaeans of the Bronze Age or from wonder at the imposing structures they had left behind them. Homer, living in the Iron Age, seemed to think of the Trojan heroes as Bronze Age warriors, since he gave them bronze weapons, although he anachronistically described one of them as being iron-hearted. The two poems that are said to be by Homer, the *Iliad* (so-called because Ilium was established on the site of ancient Troy) and the *Odyssey*, are unquestionably the greatest of the epics that remain, but they do not tell the whole story of the war and the warriors' return from it, even though they allude to events outside their narrative framework.

The *Iliad* is centred on the hero Achilles and deals with a period of just over fifty days towards the end of the ten-year war, ending before the sack of Troy. A later collection of epic poems, known as the Epic Cycle, dealt with the events leading up to the opening of the *Iliad* and took up the story where Homer left off, recounting not only the sack of Troy but the return to their homes of Greek heroes other than Odysseus. In some cases these add different or later versions of events. Only fragments of them remain, but a summary has fortunately survived. There is sufficient space here to give merely a brief outline of the events of the war; its importance to

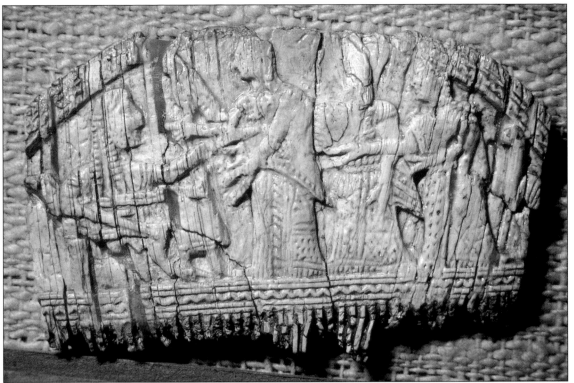

Greek audiences across several centuries may be guessed at by the hundreds of illustrations they made of it that still survive.

As so often in Greek myths, early events in the lives of some of the participants are crucial to what followed and may, in some cases, have been added at a later stage by way of explanation. There are early warnings in the lives of three people central to the story: Achilles, the Greek hero; Paris, the Trojan seducer, and Helen, the most beautiful woman in Greece, who was seduced.

Achilles was the son of a sea divinity, a Nereid called Thetis. Both Zeus and Poseidon desired her, but feared to mate with her because an oracle had said that her son would be more powerful than his father. They jointly encouraged a mortal, Peleus, to marry her, against her will. The gods attended the wedding, during which Strife threw a golden apple to the ground, saying it was 'for the fairest', an act that was to have important consequences. Disappointed of an immortal father for her child, Thetis tried to make the baby immortal: she is said to have held him either in a fire, to burn out his mortality, or in the River Styx, but the heel by which she held him remained untreated and therefore vulnerable. She took him to Cheiron to be brought up with other heroes and he soon excelled in the arts of war.

Paris was the son of the Trojan king, Priam. When Paris was born his mother dreamed that she was giving birth to a flaming torch and Priam was warned that this meant his baby son would cause the destruction of the city. Paris was therefore exposed to death on a mountainside, but he was rescued and brought up by shepherds. He became a shepherd himself, and was admired for his handsome looks and his courageous defence of his animals.

Paris lived a secluded life on Mount Ida, so when Hermes needed someone to judge who was the fairest of the three goddesses disputing their right to the golden apple he chose Paris, who was personable, yet sufficiently remote from events not to feel threatened by disputes among the gods. Hermes escorted Hera, Athena and Aphrodite to Mount Ida. As Paris looked at the goddesses in turn, each tried to influence his choice by offering him a gift: Hera offered power, Athena skill as a warrior, and Aphrodite the love of the most beautiful woman in the world. He judged Aphrodite to be the fairest and Hera and Athena became his undying enemies.

Some time later, Paris went to Troy, where he chanced to enter an athletic contest and win every event he entered. Inquiries were made, his identity revealed and he was accepted back by his father, Priam, into the royal family of Troy.

The most beautiful woman in the world at that time was Helen of Greece. Her beauty was probably inherited from her parents since her birth resulted from the rape of her beautiful mother, Leda, by Zeus who had disguised himself as a swan to trick her into submission. When Helen was old enough, all the kings and princes in Greece sought to marry her and seemed likely to fight each other for her. Some stories say that it was Odysseus who suggested the plan that she should choose her own husband and that all the suitors should then respect her choice and come to the help of her husband if she were ever abducted. Helen chose as her husband Menelaus, the rich king of Sparta. Her sister, Clytemnestra, was already married to Agamemnon, the great king of Mycenae.

The destinies of all these people began to intertwine when Paris visited Sparta, where Helen and Menelaus lived happily together with their children. He abducted Helen and took her back with him to Troy. Menelaus accordingly called upon all Helen's former suitors to mount an expedition against distant Troy to recapture Helen. Most joined him immediately, but some were reluctant. Odysseus had to be tricked into going. Thetis and Peleus knew that their son, Achilles, was fated to die if he went to Troy, and they tried to conceal him in female disguise among the women of Skyros: but when Odysseus and Diomedes came to Skyros and made a call to arms, Achilles betrayed his presence by instantly seizing some weapons.

At last, the huge fleet was ready to set off from Aulis under the leadership of great Agamemnon, but the wind would not blow. Urged by a soothsayer, and much against his will, Agamemnon sent for his daughter, Iphigenia, and sacrificed her on an altar there. The longed-for wind sprang up, but his wife, Clytemnestra, never forgave him.

There are many stories of delays on the way to Troy, and of raiding parties along the coast. Finally, the ships arrived and were drawn up on the beach in view of the city. The Greeks and Trojans could reach no agreement about Helen. Troy had impregnable walls that had been built by Poseidon. For nine years the Greeks attacked neighbouring supporters of the Trojans and cut off supplies to the city. They occasionally skirmished with warriors who ventured out of the city, but the situation remained at stalemate. The gods took sides in the war, with Hera and Athena supporting the Greeks particularly strongly because of their animus against Paris, the Trojan. In the tenth year, as had been foretold, matters came to a head. This is the point at which Homer takes up the story.

(Berlin) An Attic red-figure cup shows Achilles binding the wounded arm of Patroclos, who sits on his shield, baring his teeth in pain.

Agamemnon, the commander of the Greek army, had taken a woman called Chryseis as part of his spoil after a battle in which Achilles had fought particularly bravely. The father of Chryseis, who was a priest, begged for her to be ransomed, and called down a plague on the Greek camp when he was refused. Agamemnon therefore gave her up but, to compensate himself, seized Briseis, a female prisoner who had been given to Achilles, and of whom Achilles had become fond. Achilles was furious at this insult and vowed that neither he nor his Thessalian soldiers would fight again in the war. He withdrew to his camp in spite of a visit from the other Greek leaders, who pleaded with him and promised to return Briseis and compensate him generously.

Without Achilles, their ablest fighter, the Greeks were driven back to their ships by the Trojans, who were led by Priam's eldest son, Hector. Even the hero Ajax (Aias), with his strength and staunch courage, could not stop the Trojans. Achilles' dearest friend, Patroclos, begged that he might borrow both Achilles' soldiers and his armour in order to terrorize the Trojans on the following day. He fought bravely indeed but Hector killed him, with the help of Apollo, and took the armour of Achilles for himself. Achilles was almost mad with grief at the death of Patroclos and vowed to return to the battle at once. His mother, Thetis, persuaded Hephaestus to make him new armour that night, and the next day Achilles swept into battle. He was inspired by rage and displayed an *aristeia*, or individual valour, that destroyed all before him. At the end of a day of carnage, he met and killed Hector in single combat and dragged the body behind his chariot back to the Greek camp.

A great funeral was held for Patroclos, which included funeral games and elaborate ceremonies. In revenge for his death, Achilles continued to defile the body of Hector, dragging it round the walls of the city each day; then he left it to rot in the open air. Hector's grief-stricken father, Priam, was safely escorted by Hermes through the enemy lines to Achilles' tent, where his pleading at last moved

(British Museum) The Greek hero Achilles fights the Trojan Hector on this vase from Athens, c.490 BC.

Achilles to return the body for decent burial. The *Iliad* ends with Hector's funeral in Troy.

After this a number of allies came to the aid of Troy, including the Amazons and the Ethiopians, whose leaders were also killed by Achilles. Achilles had always known, however, that if he went to Troy he was destined to die there. It was an arrow shot from the bow of Paris, and guided by the hand of Apollo, that penetrated the unprotected place in his heel and killed him. He loss was mourned sorrowfully by the Greeks.

Some other method than valour was now needed to defeat the city. Some say Odysseus planned the stratagem of the wooden horse, others that it was the idea of the craftsman, Epeius, who constructed it. Once the horse was built, a picked group of Greek warriors climbed inside it, including the terrified Epeius who, according to some stories, was put near the door to manage the fastening. The Greek fleet then sailed round the coast out of sight, leaving one man, Sinon, behind.

The Trojans captured Sinon, who pretended that he had been intended as a sacrificial victim to obtain a wind from the gods, but had been hastily abandoned when the wind needed by the fleet sprang up spontaneously. He said the Greeks had made the horse as an offering to Athena, whose favour they felt they had lost recently, and they had made it too large to be taken through the city gates into Troy, because its presence there would protect the city. If it was left outside, Troy would fall.

Cassandra, the seer whose prophecies were doomed never to be believed, warned the Trojans that the entry of the horse would mean the destruction of the city. Laocoön, a priest of Poseidon, hurled a spear at the horse and said that he feared the Greeks, even when they brought gifts. He went to make a sacrifice on the shore; at this, two huge serpents surged out of the sea and strangled him and his young sons. The Trojans interpreted this as an omen that Laocoön was wrong, and immediately dragged the horse into the city, pulling down part of the wall in order to do so. Helen guessed that there was something amiss, and walked round the horse, speaking softly to each of the heroes in turn, mimicking the voices of their wives. Odysseus had to prevent them physically from answering her.

At night, Sinon signalled to the fleet, which

returned to Troy. The Greek warriors let themselves down from the horse and opened the city gates to their comrades from the ships. The men and children of Troy, and some of the women, were horribly slaughtered; the remaining women were taken as slaves and concubines, although some stories say that Menelaus rescued Helen. Old King Priam was murdered at an altar in the courtyard of his palace. Only Aeneas, the son of Aphrodite, escaped with his father and his son. The city was burned to the ground.

There are many stories of the difficult journeys undertaken by the Greek heroes on their return to their own lands, and few are happy. The return of Agamemnon, which was particularly tragic, will be described in the next chapter. Only Nestor, a good and wise old warrior, had a quick and easy journey home to Pylos to a quiet and contented life.

The return of Odysseus to Ithaca is recounted, largely in flash-back, in the *Odyssey*, which is so different in character from the *Iliad* as to have made many

scholars insist that the two poems are by different authors. Odysseus had the great advantage of being assisted throughout his journey by Athena, but Poseidon, the sea-god, was hostile to him and vented his hostility in savage storms. Odysseus had been told that he would be away from his home for twenty years altogether if he went to Troy, which is why he had been reluctant to go. He had another ten years to endure when he set off for home after the sack of Troy.

He and his crew began by raiding the Cicones, who killed many of them. A violent storm then took them to the land of the Lotus-eaters, who persuaded a number of his men to eat the lotus fruit, which made them forget their homes and friends and want nothing but to stay and eat more. Odysseus removed some men by force, and they sailed next to the fertile island of the Cyclopes, where many sheep and goats grazed. The Cyclopes were monsters, each of whom had one eye in the middle of his forehead.

Odysseus disembarked with a few men and went

to visit the Cyclops, Polyphemus, who was a son of Poseidon. As his cave was empty, the men made free with his food and waited for his return. When Polyphemus returned for the night with his sheep he closed the entrance to the cave with a huge rock, and dined on two of the men he found there. He had another two for breakfast, and went out again, closing the cave behind him with the rock that no human could move. While he was out, Odysseus sharpened a strong stake. Polyphemus ate two more men that night, but also drank deeply of some powerful wine. While he was asleep, the men heated the stake in the fire then drove it into his one eye. Polyphemus cried out for help, but Odysseus had told him that his name was Nobody, so the giant was ignored when, in response to enquiries from outside about his screams, he cried out 'Nobody is hurting me!' When Polyphemus opened the cave and let his sheep out in the morning, he felt their backs blindly, but could not tell that Odysseus and his men had lashed themselves beneath the bellies of the sheep. As Odysseus reached his ship, he shouted out his real name in triumph, and Polyphemus called upon his father Poseidon either to prevent Odysseus from reaching home, or to let him arrive there alone and find great trouble awaiting him.

The ship next reached the island of Aiolia whose king, Aiolos, was ruler of the winds. When Odysseus left, the king gave him a good wind that would drive his ship straight home to Ithaca, then enclosed some other winds in a tightly-tied bag, which he also gave him. After several days' sailing in the right direction, Odysseus fell asleep and his men opened the bag, thinking it might contain treasure. Contrary winds rushed out and blew the ship back to Aiolia. The king was angry, so they made for another island, which proved to be the home of the Laistrygonians. They were cannibals and they destroyed all the ships except Odysseus' own, and ate all the crews but his.

Odysseus sailed the remaining ship to the island of Aiaia where the enchantress Circe, the aunt of Medea, lived. The crew explored the island in two parties; one group came upon the home of Circe. She gave them food and drink and by doing so turned them into pigs, who nevertheless retained their human sensibilities. When Odysseus heard of this, from one of the group who had refused her hospitality and escaped, he went to their aid. Hermes met him and gave him a herb called Moly, an antidote to Circe's drugs, and told him how to master the enchantress by making love to her. Odysseus was able to persuade her to turn the pigs back into men and promise not to harm them again. Odysseus then stayed happily with Circe for a year.

When his crew urged him to depart, Circe told him that he must visit the dead in the Underworld and

consult the ghost of the blind prophet Teireisias in order to find how to get home. Although appalled at the prospect, Odysseus set sail across the river Ocean and found his way to the Underworld. He made libations and a sacrifice. The souls of the dead came in a throng to drink the sacrificial blood, but he managed to consult Teireisias about his journey. Odysseus was told that his wife, Penelope, was being besieged in Ithaca by many suitors who wanted her to choose one of them as a husband to reign in his place now that they

presumed him to be dead. He talked with, but could not embrace, the souls of some of his family, and of Achilles who had died at Troy and Agamemnon who had been killed on his return to Mycenae.

He saw men who were being punished in Hades for their impiety to the gods: Sisyphus who was condemned endlessly to push up a hill a great stone that endlessly fell back again, and Tantalus who stood in a pool that receded when he wanted to drink, and above whose head were bunches of fruit that withdrew as he

tried to grasp them. He even saw the ghost of the hero Heracles, but then he fled as hordes of spirits surrounded him. He was now free to return to Circe's island, and she gave him some useful advice about the next stage of his journey.

The first hazard Odysseus and his crew had to pass was the island of the Sirens, bird-like women who sang so enchantingly from the rocks that sailors rowed towards them and smashed their boats. Having been advised by Circe, Odysseus stopped the ears of his

KIRKA

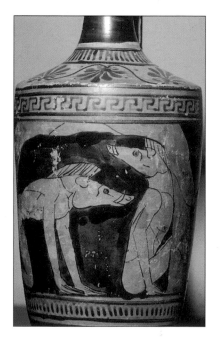

men with wax so that they could not hear the song and caused himself to be tied to the mast so that he could not steer towards the ravishing song, although he ached to do so.

Then they had to pass between Scylla and Charybdis. In order to avoid the deadly whirlpool, Charybdis, Odysseus chose to go closer to Scylla. She was a six-headed monster who waited concealed in a cave high on a rock; in spite of Odysseus's preparedness, she snatched six men from his ship as it passed beneath her rock.

The remaining men were utterly weary and depressed and insisted on anchoring at the next island. This was Thrinakie, where Apollo kept his sacred herds of cattle, and both Circe and Teireisias had insisted that Odysseus should avoid it. He made his men promise not to eat the cattle, but they were delayed there by a storm that raged for a month so that their provisions ran out, and when Odysseus was away one day the men slaughtered some of the cattle, made sacrifices to the gods, and ate the meat. The gods were angry. They sent a lull in the storm, which tempted the crew to cast off; once the ship was at sea, they sent a mighty storm that destroyed the ship and all its crew except for Odysseus himself. He clung to some wreckage and drifted for ten days until he found himself cast ashore on the island of Calypso.

He became Calypso's lover and, lacking a ship, stayed with her for seven years, although his desire to return home grew stronger all the time. He daily mourned his inability to depart from the island. Sympathetic Athena finally sent Hermes to persuade Calypso to give him the materials with which to construct a raft, and also food and drink for his journey. Some time after Odysseus had set sail, however, Poseidon sent a storm that destroyed the raft. The sea-nymph, Ino, came to his rescue by giving him a veil to wrap round himself while he swam for the nearest shore. After swimming for two days and nights he arrived naked and exhausted at the mouth of a river, and threw Ino's veil back into the sea for her. He was on the shore of Phaicia.

He was discovered the next morning by Nausicaa, daughter of the king, who had come down to the shore with her women to wash clothes. While she found him some clothes, he covered his nakedness with a leafy branch. She led him back gently to the palace, where he was received hospitably and given generous gifts. The king sent him home in one of the special ships of the Phaicians that could travel very swiftly, but which Poseidon turned into stone on its arrival in Ithaca.

Odysseus did not at first recognize Ithaca, but Athena met him and showed him where he was. Then she disguised him as an old beggar so that he could observe events in his kingdom without being recognized. He met some of his former servants and found that they were still loyal to his memory, especially his swineherd, Eumaeus. Athena removed his disguise for long enough for him to be recognized by his son Telemachus, who welcomed him with joy and relief.

His old dog, Argos, recognized him even in his beggarly disguise, and died happily, having seen him once again.

Then Odysseus approached his wife, Penelope, who treated him kindly as she would have done any beggar. He discovered that she was being driven to distraction by the suitors who had taken up residence in the palace and were eating and drinking as though they were at home. She had delayed making a decision by telling them that she must finish weaving a shroud for the father of Odysseus before she married again. She wove this all day, then unpicked the work at night, but her trick had been discovered. The disguised Odysseus won her confidence sufficiently to persuade her to tell the suitors that she would marry the one who could string her husband's great bow and send an arrow from it through twelve axe-heads set up in a line.

The competition was held the next day. None of the suitors could find the strength or expertise necessary to bend the bow and string it. Odysseus, still disguised as a beggar, asked to try. He was mocked, but finally allowed to do so. He handled the bow easily, as one accustomed to it, strung it, and shot his first arrow straight through the line of axe-heads.

The suitors were amazed, but then they were dismayed because Odysseus turned his arrows on them. He was joined in his attack by Telemachus and Eumaeus and assisted by Athena. The suitors were killed and order was restored.

Penelope tested his identity by asking her woman servant to move the bed from the room she had once shared with Odysseus. Only Odysseus could have known that the bed was immoveable, since he had himself constructed it round a living olive tree. Once Penelope saw that he knew this, she recognized that he was indeed Odysseus and welcomed him home with joy.

CHAPTER SEVEN
THE ROYAL HOUSES OF ARGOLIS AND THEBES

The cycles of myths about two ruling dynasties have special significance for us because of their treatment by the dramatists of the fifth century BC. In early historical times, Argos supplanted Mycenae and Tiryns as the chief centre of Argolis, and it may have been then that the myths of the Argolid rulers, descended from Pelops, were developed. Myths about the Theban ruling family, descended from Cadmus, were similarly brought together and embellished. Much later, the playwrights Aeschylus, Sophocles and Euripides refined the stories and gave them not only dramatic power but lasting value. Their plays show how the lives of individual men and women are influenced by the actions of their forbears, how they react emotionally and morally to situations that are forced upon them, and how they try to square their actions with their perception of their duty to the gods. Thus, the dramatists took primitive and barbaric material and made sense of it for their more enlightened world.

The myths of the Argolid family, the Pelopidai, begin with Tantalus, a king of Lydia, who lived happily and was at one with the gods, even receiving them as guests. One day, however, as an ill-judged test of their discernment, he served them the flesh of his son, Pelops. The gods drove him to eternal punishment in Hades for this hideous act, but they restored Pelops to life.

Pelops moved into Greece, where the Peloponnese still bears his name. He won his wife Hippodamia from her father, the King of Pisa, by taking up his challenge to a chariot race; in order to win, Pelops secretly arranged that the wheels should fall from the king's chariot. He thus won the race and a wife, but the king was killed and Pelops' guilt was inherited by the next generation.

Pelops and Hippodamia had many sons, among them Atreus and Thyestes, who were notorious from youth for their mutual discord. When Pelops sent them into exile, they went to their sister's husband, Eurystheus, King of Mycenae. When he died an oracle said that one of Pelops' sons should have his throne. So began a long and devious struggle between them, which ended when Atreus discovered that his wife, Aerope, was secretly the mistress of Thyestes. He killed her; then he killed Thyestes' sons and invited Thyestes to a feast, at which he served him their roasted flesh.

Thyestes asked the oracle how he might take revenge on his brother, and was told that only a son of his begotten on his own daughter, Pelopia, could do it. He took the oracle literally, disguised himself and raped her. Pelopia, finding herself pregnant, married her widowed uncle Atreus, and Thyestes' new son, Aegisthus, grew up thinking he was the son of Atreus. When Aegisthus discovered the truth, he killed Atreus after cursing him and all his descendants.

The true sons of Atreus were Agamemnon and Menelaus. Agamemnon became ruler of Mycenae and married Clytemnestra; Menelaus ruled Sparta and married Helen, Clytemnestra's sister. As we have seen, both kings were away in Troy for more than ten years. Clytemnestra hated her husband who

(Capitoline Museum, Rome) Portrait bust of Aeschylus. Aeschylus (c.525-456 BC) was the first of the three great dramatists of the Classical period, the others being Sophocles and Euripides, and he is the only one from whom a complete trilogy of tragedies survives, telling a continuous story. He said of the writers of his period that 'We are all eating crumbs from the great table of Homer.'

had sacrificed their daughter, Iphigenia, in order to obtain a propitious wind for the Trojan fleet. She and Agamemnon had other children: a son called Orestes and daughters called Electra and Chrysothemis.

While Agamemnon was away in Troy Clytemnestra took Aegisthus, the son of Thyestes, as her lover. Perceiving the danger of this situation to Agamemnon's heirs, Electra, the eldest daughter, smuggled her young brother Orestes away to safety in Phocis. Some stories say that she herself was forced into marriage with a peasant so that Agamemnon's royal line should not continue. When, after ten years, watch-fires flared across the landscape to announce the return of Agamemnon from Troy, the lovers agreed to murder him. Clytemnestra met her husband with sweet ceremony and prepared a bath for him. While he was helpless in his bath, she trapped him in a net and killed him brutally with an axe.

Guilt for this murder passed to the next generation, for when Orestes grew up it was his duty to avenge his father. Summoned by Electra, he returned secretly seven years later, with a friend called Pylades, and left clues of his presence for his sister at an altar where she worshipped. Electra persuaded him that he must kill Clytemnestra and Aegisthus, in spite of his reluctance. He did the deed but then, as a punishment for his matricide, the Furies pursued him wherever he went. In some stories he travelled the world in a desperate attempt to escape them. In his play the *Eumenides* (The Furies), Aeschylus chooses, rather, to show that Athena brought Orestes to Athens to appear before Apollo at a court of law, the Areopagus, where Orestes was 'cleared of the charge of blood' and allowed to go home. Athena persuaded the vengeful Furies to become instead the Eumenides, 'Kindly Ones', who brought benefits to

102

(British Museum) A bronze representation of one of the Erinyes, or Furies, minor goddesses who were born from the drops of blood spilt on the earth at the castration of Ouranus. These winged creatures tortured to madness those who had committed serious offences, especially against the family, such as Orestes' murder of his mother.

Athens. The cycle of bloody and revengeful acts was thus brought to a close by a merciful decision.

The city of Thebes in Boeotia also had its cycle of myths. These began with Agenor, a king of Phoenicia. His daughter, Europa, was abducted by Zeus in the shape of a bull, who carried her on his back to Crete. Agenor sent his sons to search for her. After much travelling, his son Cadmus went to the

Delphic oracle to ask for help and was told to stop searching for Europa but instead to follow a cow that he would see in Phocis; at the place where the cow sat down to rest he should build a city. He obeyed, and built the city that became Thebes. He killed a serpent, a son of Ares, that he found guarding a near-by spring and, needing men to people his town, he sowed the serpent's teeth in the ground. Armed war-

riors sprang up, but they were too many and too fierce, so he threw a stone into their midst and, each suspecting the other, they fought until only five men remained. These became the ancestors of the leading Theban families, whose descendants continued to call themselves spartoi, or 'sown men' into historical times.

Cadmus married Harmonia, the daughter of

Aphrodite's affair with Ares, at a wedding attended by the gods. We have already encountered some of the couple's daughters in other myths: Semele bore Dionysus to Zeus; Autonoë was the mother of Actaeon, and Agaue became the unfortunate queen who tore her son Pentheus to pieces when he tried to stop the spread of the cult of Dionysus.

Cadmus's male descendants became kings of

(National Archaeological Museum, Palermo) Metope from a Temple at Selinunte, 6th century BC, showing Europa sitting on the back of Zeus, who has disguised himself as a bull. She holds on to his horn as he rushes her away from Phoenicia to Crete.

(National Archaeological Museum, Athens) A Hellenistic relief showing Oedipus preparing to answer the question set by the Sphinx. She is a winged female creature with the head and breasts of a woman and the legs and body of a lion.

Thebes in their turn. His great-grandson, Laius, married Jocasta, who is known by the name Epikaste in earlier versions of the story. Laius was warned by an oracle that any son of his would be destined to kill his father and marry his mother. Therefore when Jocasta had a son Laius pinned the baby's feet together and had him abandoned on Mount Cithaeron.

The baby was found by a shepherd who took it to his master, Polybus, the King of Corinth who, being childless, adopted it as his son, calling him

Oedipus, or 'Swollen Foot'. As a young man, Oedipus visited the oracle at Delphi, where he was told that he was destined one day to kill his father and marry his mother. He determined never to return to Corinth, to the couple he thought were his parents, but set off to find some other home where he might escape his destiny.

One day, as he arrived at a crossroads, he was almost crushed by a chariot. In the tussle that followed, he overturned the chariot and killed its passenger. He went on, however, and came to Thebes.

The city was plagued at that time by a monstrous winged creature, part-woman and part-lion, who sat on a precipice and cast to their death all those who could not answer the riddle she set them. This was: 'What is it that walks upon four legs, upon two legs and upon three legs?' Oedipus courageously went to encounter her and found the answer to the question – it was Man, who crawls on all fours as a baby, goes upright in his prime, and uses a stick as a third leg when he is old and lame. Defeated at last, the Sphinx threw herself from her rock.

Laius, the king of Thebes, had failed to return from a journey, and was presumed dead. Oedipus was considered the saviour of Thebes because he had defeated the Sphinx so Jocasta gave him the kingdom by marrying him. They lived contentedly together and had two sons, Eteocles and Polyneices, and two daughters, Antigone and Ismene.

In time, however, a terrible plague laid low the citizens of Thebes, and the crops failed. Jocasta's brother, Creon, went to the oracle at Delphi and returned with the message that the plague would be lifted only when the murderer of Jocasta's first husband, Laius, had been found; the unknown man was in Thebes and was the source of pollution.

In his play *Oedipus Tyrannus*, Sophocles shows in almost unbearable sequence how Oedipus gradually unravels the true story of his own birth and his killing of his real father, Laius, at the crossroads. When he found that he had not escaped the oracle, but had indeed killed his father and married his mother, he blinded himself with Jocasta's brooches because he was no longer fit to see the light of day. Jocasta hanged herself. In Sophocles' version of later events, in *Oedipus at Colonus*, Oedipus left Thebes and went to Colonus, guided by his daughter Antigone, and ended his days by vanishing from a sacred grove in a miraculous yet peaceful fashion.

The story of Thebes was not yet played out, however. His incestuous union left its mark on his children. The two sons of Oedipus, Eteocles and Polyneices, both wanted to rule in Thebes, and agreed that each should rule for one year at a time. Eteocles would not give up the rule at the end of his year, however, and Polyneices collected support from Argos and, with his companions, mounted a failed expedition against the city, known as 'The Seven Against Thebes'. When the two brothers finally met in single combat, they killed each other. Creon, their uncle, took charge of the kingdom, and refused to allow Antigone to bury Polyneices. Greek custom demanded that bodies should be buried in order that the spirits of their owners should find rest. Antigone therefore defied Creon and buried her brother. Creon condemned her to death for this, and Creon's son Haimon, who was to have married her, chose to end his life too.

The words of the Chorus at the end of Sophocles' play, *Antigone*, show clearly the relation between men and the just gods, the impossibility of escaping what they have decreed, and the foolishness of opposing them with pride: 'Of happiness the crown and chiefest part is wisdom, and to hold the gods in awe. That is the law that, seeing the stricken heart of pride brought down, we learn when we are old.' That lesson can be learned from most of the myths. No one is forced into any particular belief and minor irregularities of behaviour may be overlooked; the gods, in any case, do not behave very differently from imperfect humans, but are gods and must be respected and not challenged. That was the wise way to live.

INDEX